B00 25015
17.95 -1436

P9-AFX-098

THE YACHTSMAN'S EMERGENCY HANDBOOK

Revised Edition

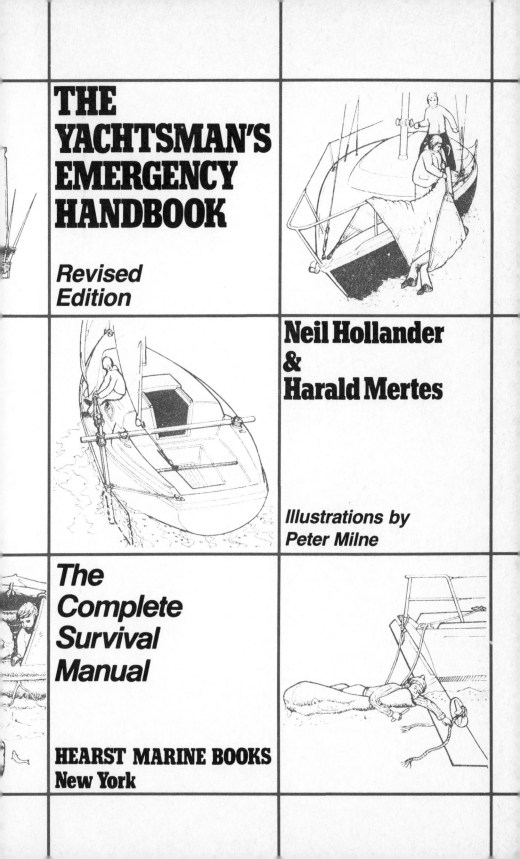

Neil Hollander & Harald Mertes

Illustrations by Peter Milne

The Complete Survival Manual

HEARST MARINE BOOKS
New York

To Gilbert and Heinz
who advised us:

*'When in danger or in doubt,
Sail in circles, scream and shout!'*

Copyright © 1980 by Neil Hollander and Harald Mertes
The American edition copyright © 1980 by Hearst Books
The revised edition copyright © 1986 by Hearst Marine Books

All rights reserved. No part of this book may be reproduced or utilized in any form
or by any means, electronic or mechanical, including photocopying, recording or
by any information storage and retrieval system, without permission in writing
from the Publisher. Inquiries should be addressed to Permissions Department,
William Morrow and Company, Inc., 105 Madison Ave., New York, N.Y. 10016.

Library of Congress Cataloging-in-Publication Data

Hollander, Neil.
  The yachtsman's emergency handbook.

  Includes index.
  1. Boats and boating—Safety measures—Handbooks,
manuals, etc.   2. Yachts and yachting—Safety measures
—Handbooks, manuals, etc.   I. Mertes, Harald.
II. Title.
GV777.55.H64   1986   797.1'028'9   86-12070
ISBN 0-688-06610-0

Printed in the United States of America

FIRST REVISED EDITION

1 2 3 4 5 6 7 8 9 10

Introduction

The idea for this book arrived during a storm – a Force 9 gale in the Gulf of Lions. Like many storms one encounters at sea, foam and fury suddenly seemed to come from nowhere. Rumbling black clouds raced across the sky and what had been a tranquil four-day passage from Sète to Ibiza was quickly twisted into a mistral struggle. Swimming suits off – oilskins on, genoa down – trysail up, fishing lines in – sea anchor out.

As the seas rose higher and higher, our overaged cutter began to shudder and creak. Her timbers started to work and, to our horror, caulking fell out like dandruff.

A plank separated from the stem. Then another.

The backstay parted.

All three bilge pumps packed up.

So did the engine, roller reefing and the galley stove.

A hurried search through a shelf of soggy yachting books yielded no quick solutions – in fact, no solutions at all. The emphasis was clearly on the 'buy' and 'buy not' and the 'do' and 'do not'. For some reason, the vital 'when' and 'if' were hard to find. With chaos whirling about us, there wasn't time to skim through densely printed pages of anecdote and theory, searching for bits of emergency advice.

Unfortunately, we were on our own, and that was by no means comforting. Angry seas inspire little confidence. To make matters worse, at that moment in our sailing lives there was too much we didn't know and hadn't tried. Yet, somehow – certainly more by luck than by experience – our guesses outweighed our mistakes, and our instincts kept us afloat and alive. Jury-rigged, jury-sailed and jury-fed we listed into Ibiza a week later.

Not everything was repaired at sea, of course. Far from it. However, we did manage to keep the boat in what might be generously called a 'a serviceable order'. It was only later we realized that that was exactly what we should have done.

Since then, wherever we have sailed – the Atlantic, Caribbean and Pacific – we have made a habit of noting down bits and pieces of emergency experience; our own, and also those of other yachtsmen which were passed to us over mooring lines and bars: tips, shortcuts, the makeshift and make-do, the impractical essential and the essential impractical.

The result – this book – is by no means complete, nor is it a panacea, but we do hope it will point someone in trouble in the right direction – if not with a solution, then at least with a few hints as to where he might look for one. The procedures and signals we give conform to the international rules of the road, which differ from the rules for inland waters.

We have tried to keep the text as pragmatic and terse as possible, maintaining the perspective that whatever the emergency – dismasting, engine failure, grounding or a man overboard – it is occurring at the moment. The immediate, crucial question is: What must be done? Now! First!

We have left out such actions as 'Call all hands on deck!' 'Put on lifejackets!' or 'Tend to the injured!' as they are – we should hope – too obvious to mention. Our concern has been with the less obvious – the difficult decision and the logical – or in some cases apparently illogical – actions that follow.

For these, we have drawn freely from the large storehouse of accumulated knowledge, that which lives in the minds and hearts of yachtsmen and sailors and also that which is filed on dusty library shelves.

Hence, we have many people to thank.

Certainly, without them this book would never be.

Acknowledgments

Tom Streithorst (*Alkatraz*), Charles Malcolm (*Ancela*), J. H. Plettenberg (*Andromeda*), Chantal Izard (*Audonien*), Nigel Dalton (*Blackbeard*), Liljana de Pauli (*Chica*), Jesse and Stephen (*Double Eagle*), Brian McGarry and Joe Menell (*Fiona*), Bob Taylor (*Freedom*), Tony Badger (*Gaucho*), Herbert Gossmann (*Jonas*), Helmut and Anne Möhrmann (*Kleiner Bär*), Simone Darmon (*La Marie Garlande*), Heinz Tenbrinck (*La Paloma*), James Irvitie (*Mathew*), Rolando Soto (*Media Luna*), Paul and Martha Setram (*Mercedes*), Howard Benett (*Nana*), Alain Relmy (*Nayla*), Kurt M. Englebert (*Peer Gynt*), Herman Biasotti (*Sol*), Ferdl and Susi Kassler (*Venceremos*).

Our medical advisors were Nurse Mary Jo Nelson, Dr. Henry Campion of the American Hospital of Paris, and Dr. Robert Corwin, Dr. Günther Dötsch, Dr. Judith Jones, Dr. Max Krämer and Dr. Adolf Keuser of Koblenz.

Many people aided us in ways too numerous to mention: Sabine Bäcker, Irmela Brender, Don Manuel Campos, Nadia Christensen, Otmar Dills, the de Pauli family, Maggie Hemingway, Dennis Ing, Lilly Libedinsky, Stephen Paul, Malcolm Robson, Charles Roth, Joachim and Brigitte Scheid, Norman Stokle, the Tepa family of Bora Bora, and Liz, Penny, Elspeth, and Sally of the Cruising Association.

Brookes & Gatehouse, Citizens of the Sea, Cruising Association, Electronic Laboratories, Günter Schleich, Ocean Cruising Club, RFD Inflatables, Rhein-Mosel Yacht Club, Switlik Parachute Company.

Rainy Day Reading

This chapter should be read on a rainy day. It contains the critical first steps to ensure the safety of your passengers and boat. It will discuss potential hazards and enable you to fend them off with proper equipment and procedures. In the main text of *Yachtsman's Emergency Handbook* you will find more than 500 useful cures for standard and unusual problems (Yes, it has all happened before). These are the essential second steps to handle hazards on your boat: to be used as a problem crops up—which inevitably happens. Like the problems, some of the solutions are centuries old. They are tried and true and important for the boat owner to know. New standards to prevent accidents and new techniques for coping with mishaps are equally important. In this chapter the following first steps are discussed:

• Risk management as a concept
• Standards for boat safety
• Predictable hazards and how to avoid them
• Inspection procedures

Risk Management

There are two ways to look at accidents at sea:

1 – Trying never to have an accident, and
2 – The best way to have an emergency

Sooner or later, something unexpected happens. This principle of Mother Nature at Sea is much older than Murphy's famous law. There is one advantage in the nautical world: You can cope with emergencies if you have proper equipment and tools, proper training in essential skills of seamanship, and a mental attitude that you have trained and tested. As Charles F. Chapman said in an early edition of his noted book, *Piloting, Seamanship & Small Boat Handling,* "Safety at sea is conditioned, not upon the caprice of chance or the elements, but upon the boat and the person responsible for her." These points apply whether you are operating a small powerboat on a lake, sailing a hot racer-cruiser in an overnight, or making a solo transoceanic passage in a rugged sloop.

In the middle third of this century some of the toughest yachtsmen became some of the wisest. In the prewar boating era, lifelines on small cruising sailboats were relatively unknown; today they are standard. The old salts didn't think to wear life jackets when going on deck in bad weather; today the young salts know that the hazard of going into the water at night without a PFD is similar to the hazard of leaving an airplane in flight without a parachute. Even the toughest powerboat racers are now accepting this idea of risk management. Safety harnesses, fail-safe controls, and hazard-free operating methods are all part of the same approach.

Standards for Boat Safety

The standards for boat construction and equipment worked out by safety councils, a few top naval architects, the U.S. Coast Guard, some of the tougher racing groups, and insurance organizations are worth knowing about. As a boat owner you aren't likely to need a complete understanding of the engineering aspects of all these standards. However, being aware of them will help you to outfit and operate your boat properly.

Of the standards-making groups, the American Boat and Yacht Council is perhaps the one that has the broadest usefulness for boat owners, since its standards cover both large and small powerboats and sailboats.

A typical example from ABYC standards is the one that specifies that the top rail of a lifeline on deck shall be at least 24 inches from the deck. Anyone who has faced the dangers of a pitching deck and seas crashing aboard knows the importance of adequate lifelines. The subject is well covered in the ABYC book *Standards and Recomended Practices for Small Craft,* under the heading "Security of Personnel on Deck." This book, although technical in nature, is very useful for anyone planning voyages. Various project technical committees develop the standards, which are advisory.

There are about 65 different ABYC safety standards, covering hulls, machinery, electric systems, equipment, and engineering standards. The following indicates their scope:

Good Visibility from the Helm Position
Ventilation—Gasoline Boats
Cockpits and Scuppers
Safe Loading of Small Craft
Fastenings in Vessels
Buoyancy in the Event of Swamping

Hull Openings Between Water Line and Sheer Line
Thermal and Acoustical Insulation, Sheathing Materials, and Fire Retardant Coatings
Safe Powering of Boats

Inflatable Boats
Hydraulic Systems
Ventilation—Diesel Boats
Liquid-Cooled Marine Engines
Air-Cooled Marine Engines
Diesel Engines
Power-Transmitting Units Penetrating the Hull
Bonding of Direct Current Systems
Wiring Identification
Electrical Systems
Batteries
Hatches and Doors
Glazing Materials
Bilge Pumps
Potable Water Systems Metal
Fuel Systems
Portable Fuel Systems
Seacocks
Canoes
Exhaust Systems
Engine Mountings
Propeller Shafting
Control Systems
Steering Systems
Cathodic Protection
Lightning Protection, AC
DC Wiring Systems
Galley Stoves
Liquefied Petroleum Gas Systems

Fire-Fighting Equipment
Refrigeration and Air-Conditioning Equipment
Sewage Treatment Devices
Flammable Gas Indicators
Lifesaving Equipment
Security of Personnel on Deck
Compressed Natural Gas Systems
Aluminum Applications
Boat Measurements and Weight
Instrument Panel and Speedometer Installation
Remote Control Mounting Pads
Motor Well Dimensions
Sailboat Inboard Well Dimensions
Sailboat Auxiliary Horsepower
Ground Tackle
Boat Heating Systems
Distress Signals
Navigation Lights
Battery Chargers
Electronic Equipment
Owner's Manuals
Boat Serial Number
Horsepower Ratings
Motor Mounting Areas
Compass Installation
Oil Test Procedures
Motor Dimensions

The American Boat and Yacht Council can be contacted at P.O. Box 806, Amityville, NY 11701. The telephone number is (516) 598-0550. The membership, although predominantly manufacturers and naval architects, includes many individual boat owners.

The Coast Guard's requirements are the only ones that are legally mandatory. Some racing organizations basically say: "If you don't comply with these rules, you can't be in our race." U.S. Coast Guard requirements, however, are minimal, and most boat owners recognize this. Nevertheless, trying to substitute European Personal Flotation Devices for those approved by the U.S. Coast Guard, for example, can cause more problems than it solves.

Among the other organizations that work on standards for design or construction, in reference to safety and efficient operation, are the

Boating Industries Association–National Marine Manufacturers Association, (BIA-NMMA), the National Fire Protection Association, the Underwriters Laboratories (whose Marine Division performs tests and conducts safety investigations), and the National Association of Marine Surveyors. The Society of Automotive Engineers (SAE) and specialized publications are all sources of standards, test reports, and other kinds of helpful information or services.

The American Bureau of Shipping, Lloyd's of London, North German Lloyd's, Veritas, the various yacht-racing unions, and such groups as the Midget Ocean Racing Club or the Cruising Club of America are at times worth looking into for specific solutions.

The listing, in these pages, of the various subjects covered by marine safety standards is one indication of subjects to consider for a boat owner preparing for a voyage. But in addition to the basic safety of the boat and its equipment, there are various natural and man-made hazards to avoid, control, or face properly.

Predictable Hazards and How to Avoid Them

Lightning is a powerful and dangerous force. A boat operating on the west coast of Florida may be exposed to 80 lightning storms a year, while one on the coast of Maine may have only 10 exposures. Safety from lightning depends primarily on proper grounding of a boat's lifeline and, in the case of a sailboat, spars and rigging.

A similar danger, that of masts hitting high-tension lines that cross over waterways, requires operator care. While cruising on inland waterways, sailboat owners should have a crew member looking up and ahead for hazardous telephone and electric lines.

Fire and explosion prevention includes (a) safe installations, (b) safe procedures, (c) having adequate fire-fighting equipment installed, and (d) knowing how to put out a small fire before it becomes a large fire or leads to an explosion.

The leading causes of the 4,000 boat fires that occur each year in the United States are gasoline vapors, propane vapors, exhaust system failures, diesel fuel system failures, galley stove failures, and electrical failures.

Leaks in the gasoline line, often caused by the addition of alcohol to the fuel, which leads to the rapid deterioration of rubber and even metal fuel lines, are a principal cause of marine fires. Proper replacement of fuel line components is the safeguard. The sources of gasoline leaks are tanks, fittings, and fuel lines. In addition, the ground wire from the fuel filler deck plate should be checked.

Electronic fuel-vapor monitoring systems are another safeguard, often as important as the basic blower system in the engine area.

Correct fueling procedures, which require the cooperation of all on board the vessel, are also vital.

First, shut off all electric systems, including the blowers but not including the vapor detector.

Second, crew members should leave the boat. If this is not possible, they should leave enclosed cabin areas.

Third, all cigarettes, the galley stove, and heater fires must be extinguished.

Fourth, make sure the fuel hose nozzle is securely placed in the fuel filler opening, to prevent static electricity.

Fifth, if fuel is spilled, it should be hosed off. If it spills into the water, wait until it dissipates before starting the motor.

Sixth, check engine and tank compartments for fuel vapors before starting the blowers. Run the blowers for four minutes before starting the motor.

In the United States there are Coast Guard requirements specifying the type and number of various sizes of fire extinguishers needed on different boats. Vessels that will be operating in faraway areas should have more than the minimum, partly because replacements or refills may be difficult to get.

There are three categories of fires:

Class A fires occur in ordinary combustible materials such as wood, paper, and cloth. The quenching/cooling effect of water works by lowering the temperature below the ignition point.

Class B fires are in flammable petroleum or other products. The blanketing effect, excluding oxygen, is the means that works best on this type of fire.

Class C fires are electrical and the important characteristic of the right fire extinguisher is that it be a nonconductor.

Fire extinguishers are also classified as A, B, or C. The B type is required by law on recreational boats and is usually most convenient. Foam-type extinguishers, like water, will extinguish Type A fires, but should never be used on electrical fires. An older type of vaporizing-liquid extinguisher, using carbon tetrachloride and chlorobromo-methane, was effective. These are no longer legal, because they produce highly toxic gases.

Fire avoidance and fire-fighting procedures and techniques are as important as the equipment and its location.

The weekly inspection of fire extinguishers (and the follow-up maintenance when recharging is indicated), the training of crew members in their use, the holding of fire drills, and knowing the right way to handle a fire when it occurs are all important.

Water, applied promptly and adequately, is best for fires that do not involve fuel or grease, or electrical circuits.

Closing hatches and vents, reducing oxygen, is effective. Cutting off the fuel supply is often important.

Stopping the boat, or reducing speed, is usually indicated, so that the wind does not fan the flames. Maneuver the boat so that the fire is downwind.

Direct the fire extinguisher at the base of the flames. Remember that small extinguishers have a discharge time of only 8 to 20 seconds.

If the fire is not extinguished promptly, you may have to radio for assistance or prepare to abandon ship.

Inspection Procedures

Besides having proper equipment on a properly maintained boat, one additional step is needed: inspection. This can involve almost constant attention, including watching engine instrument gauges, hourly procedures to check the rigging, spars, and sails under difficult sailing conditions, and other maintenance procedures.

The following is meant to be a reminder of the main systems, with emphasis on things that go wrong. Check:

- Anchor lines, for chafe.
- Shackles, for tight and wired pins.
- Seacocks, that they work freely and are lubricated adequately.
- Engine and galley systems, for fuel leaks and ventilation problems. On deck, fill plates for fuel and water should be clearly marked.
- Water tanks should be checked for leaks and contamination.
- Batteries, electrical systems, and electronic equipment, for potential malfunctions.
- Rigging, sails, and spars, for chafe, broken or distorted parts, or fittings that are frozen from lack of lubrication.
- Life rafts should be stowed in canisters on deck or in their own lockers, opening on to the deck. Man Overboard Modules should be accessible and free.
- Personal Flotation Devices, for accessibility. Lights, emergency radio transmitters, EPIRBS, and whistles should be checked.

The following information is from *Piloting, Seamanship & Small Boat Handling,* by Elbert S. Maloney:

In case of collision, accident, or other casualty involving a pleasure boat, the operator must make a report if the incident results in death, an injury requiring medical treatment, the disappearance of a person from a vessel under circumstances that indicate death or injury, or if there is property damage totaling more than $200.

If death occurs within 24 hours of the accident, or a person has a reportable injury or disappears from the boat, a formal report must be made within 48 hours; otherwise, within 10 days.

Most state boating laws require that reports of boating accidents be made to a designated state office. If there is no state provision, a report must be made to the U.S. Coast Guard Officer in Charge, Marine Inspection, nearest the site of the accident.

Coast Guard regulations list the information that must be furnished. The "Boating Accident" report form, CG-3865, may be used.

In addition, a boat operator should make careful note of all the circumstances of an accident in the log, and preserve the log book in case the vessel is abandoned.

Stowage Plan

Before you set off, it is a good idea to draw a rough plan of your boat and plan your stowage.

BELOW DECK

ABOVE DECK

Abandon ship!

See also: Evacuation

Alongside a larger vessel ■ 1

If a choice exists, allow yourself to be hoisted on board, rather than climb a ladder against the ship's side.

Leave the boat from well forward or well aft of the mast so as not to be struck or tangled by the spars or rigging.

Time your moment of departure so that you leave on the crest of a wave, letting the boat fall away from you.

WARNING:

Going alongside a freighter or tanker risks being dismasted.

Into a liferaft

See: Liferaft

■ 1 *Boarding a larger vessel*

Jumping in the water

Loosen clothing.

If wearing a lifejacket, hold it down and away from your chin.

Leave from the windward side, since more than likely the boat will drift faster than you can swim.

Jump feet first, legs together, with your mouth closed. If jumping from a height, hold nose and cover mouth.

Swim clear of the boat.

If there is oil in the water

Swim underwater if possible. Keep your eyes tightly shut. When coming up for air, protect your eyes, nose and mouth with your hands as you break the surface. Use your arms to sweep away the oil, turn your back to the wind, hold your breath and dive again.

When swimming on the surface, use a rapid breast stroke to thrust the oil away from your face.

In cold water

Enter the water fully clothed.

Empty your pockets of all weights.

Do not remove boots, shoes or mittens.

If possible, tape or tightly tie wrists, waist and ankles so that water trapped inside will have a wet-suit effect. For perhaps the first quarter of an hour, clothes will provide some buoyancy and later when soaked become excellent insulation. Contrary to expectation, wet clothes in the water weigh no more than dry clothes ashore.

Float. Do *not* swim. Exercise will only increase your heat loss, thus depriving you of energy.

NOTE:

Immediately after entering the water, you will probably find it difficult to breathe normally. However, this will pass within a few minutes.

Rescue by helicopter

METHOD 1

Keep the boat on a predictable course.

Make your exit from the stern.

If possible, release the standing backstay, running backstays, and other lines that might foul the transfer.

Show a green light or flag if you are ready to leave, a red light or flag if not.

Do *not* make fast the line or wire lowered from the helicopter, and beware of electrostatic discharge from the end of the wire when it is first lowered.

Normally the helicopter will lower a harness. If not, prepare a bosun's chair.

For an emergency bosun's chair **See: Climbing the mast.**

METHOD 2

Make contact with the helicopter from a dinghy or liferaft towed astern.

Accidents

See also: Salvage

If an accident occurs

By law and custom the vessels are bound to stand by and render aid to each other and exchange the following:

Names.

Home ports.

Ports from which they have come.

Ports to which they are going.

Legal action

This can nearly always be started in the country whose flag flies on the stern of the ship being prosecuted.

U.S. and British courts allow collision actions to be brought if the guilty ship, irrespective of its nationality, is in a U.S. or British port at the time the action is brought.

French and German courts claim jurisdiction if the damaged yacht flies their flag, even though the guilty vessel may be foreign. In principle, a ship is a part of the country, and a collision with a French or German vessel is said to have occurred in either France or Germany.

NOTE:

A violation of 'The Rules of the Road' **(See: Collision)** is no longer a presumption of guilt. Courts now examine all circumstances to determine the responsibility for the accident.

Aground

On a weather shore
Back the jib with the wind abaft the beam – jibe

On a lee shore
Drop or luff all sails at once

Usually, *the easiest way off* is the same route one went on.

Start the engine

Apply moderate power. Your own wake, rolling under the stern, may lift the boat free.

WARNING:

If the tide is ebbing

There may be little time before the boat is hopelessly aground. For example, with a tidal range of 12–14ft. (3–4m.), a fall of 4in. (10cm.) in 10 minutes is not unusual. With a falling tide, unless one gets off almost immediately, it is better to prepare the boat to dry out than to waste valuable time trying to break free. **See: Drying out.**

If the tide is rising

The danger lies in being swept farther aground. Free the sheets, and take down all sail. Anchors should be set at once, and, depending on sea and weather conditions, both fore and aft. **See: Anchoring**

NOTE:

High water at night is usually slightly higher than high water during the day.

Heeling

Heeling to one side may reduce the draft and free the boat. Should the keel be stuck in mud this may also break the suction hold.

WARNING:

Boats with bilge keels should not be heeled ■ **3**. Once the boat is heeled, her draft increases.

NOTE:
The moment a heeled boat breaks free, the sails, the engine, or a bow anchor should be ready for a seaward course.

METHOD 1 Heeling with weights

Use the weight of the crew on the crosstrees, end of the boom, or hanging over the side.

Tie a weight such as an anchor, dinghy filled with water, or water cans to the end of the boom and run it out abeam. Support the boom with the main halyard attached to the boom end ■ **4**.

■ **2** *Heeling decreases the draft*

■ **3** *Heeling increases the draft*

■ **4** *Heeling with weights*

METHOD 2 Heeling with an anchor

Lay the anchor chain on the deck to list the boat.

Lay out the kedge anchor and attach its warp to the main, jib, or spinnaker halyard. Take the fall of the halyard to a winch ■ **5**.

WARNING:

Masthead fittings are not designed for lateral pull. To reduce strain, a strong line can be attached to the end of the halyard and the free end rove through a snatch block on the kedge warp, then taken to a cockpit winch ■ **5**. This will also increase the holding power of the anchor. An even less risky method, especially if your halyard is wire, is to secure a strap loosely around the mast, shackled to the main halyard. Snap a snatchblock to the strap and reeve the anchor rode in the

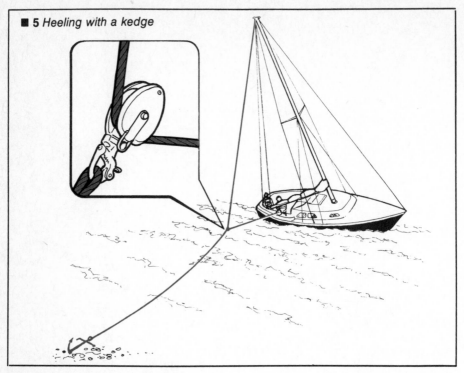

■ 5 *Heeling with a kedge*

■ 6 *Heeling with backed sails*

snatchblock. Hoist to spreaders by raising the halyard and take a strain on the anchor rode.

METHOD 3 Heeling with backed sails

Back the jib and/or mainsail thereby heeling the boat to leeward **■ 6**.

NOTE:

Without an anchor set, this method tends to push the boat farther ashore.

METHOD 4 Heeling with the aid of a towboat

Tie the towrope loosely around the mast, then hoist the bight to the spreaders with the main halyard **■ 7, 8**.

In this case do *not* pass the end of a halyard to the towboat as the strain generated by a large motorboat could easily endanger the mast.

■ **7** *Heeling with a towboat*

■ **8** *Heeling with a towboat*

NOTE:

For short fin keels

Rocking the boat back and forth and pivoting, in addition to heeling, can often slew the boat free.

Lightening the boat

Empty water and fuel tanks.

Internal ballast, spare anchors and chain can be heaved over the side, buoyed, and retrieved later.

All nonessential crew members can be moved into the dinghy.

NOTE:

Boats with long keels usually have their deepest draft aft. Consequently, moving crew and weight to the bow may be enough to shift the balance. This, combined with poling, using the engine, or pulling on a seaward anchor may be enough to free the boat.

■ **9** *Redistributing the boat's weight*

Kedging off

Set the kedge anchor from the dinghy.
See: Anchoring – A dragging anchor

Take the kedge warp to the anchor winch,
cockpit winch, or a block and tackle. **See:
Block and tackle**

Hauling off

Use the kedge anchor to heel the boat

*Use the bow anchor to haul the boat
free*

To heel the boat **(See: Heeling)** lay out
the kedge anchor and tie the warp to a
rope halyard reeved through a swivel
block attached to the face of the mast,
such as a staysail halyard or spinnaker

pole lift. Second choice would be a
spinnaker halyard, which may twist the
mast. Last choice would be to wire the
main halyard as it may be kinked and
permanently damaged.

To haul her off, lay out the bow anchor,
and tie the chain or warp to a winch or
block and tackle. If twin-keeled, secure
the towline around the keels.

Heel and pivot the boat at the same time
■ 10.

NOTE:

If two warps need to be connected, use a
Carrick bend. **See: Knots**

WARNING:

If aground on hard rock, do not try to haul
free as this could easily damage the boat.
Instead prepare to dry out. **See: Drying
out**

■ 10 *Hauling off*

Wakes and waves

The passing of another ship, especially a big one, can produce a wave large enough to free the boat momentarily.

A speedboat moving back and forth, even at low speeds, can have the same effect.

WARNING:

The boat may lift on a wake or wave and then crash down violently, possibly damaging herself or throwing the crew off balance.

Pushing and lifting

Besides lightening the boat, the muscle power of a few crew members in the water often equals a strong winch. The person in the water should be fully clothed, wearing boots or shoes and gloves. His most powerful stance is under the bows, pushing backwards and upwards with his back. With bilge keels and light displacement craft, the best place is under the quarter.

If there is no possibility of refloating the boat

See: Drying out

If the boat is in danger of breaking up

See: Scuttling

Ahull

See: Heavy weather

Aluminum repair

Leaks and holes

Repairing a small crack or tear

These can be filled with mastic, filler, cold solder, fiberglass or epoxy resin.

Repairing a larger rent

These will have to be patched.

Drill a small hole at each end of the crack to prevent it from continuing.

Cut the aluminum patch in a round or oval shape with at least 2in. (5cm.) of overlap. If necessary, for short periods of time, any metal can be used.

Slightly bevel the outside edges of the patch.

Drill holes around the edges no more than 2in. (5cm.) apart.

Shape the patch to the form of the hull with a rubber mallet.

Placing the patch on the outside of the hull is usually easier, but inside patching will permit the crack to be filled and sanded later to maintain a smooth hull form.

Clean and lightly sand the area around the hole or crack.

Using the patch as a template, mark the holes in the hull, then drill them.

Cover the inside of the patch with mastic or bedding compound.

Rivet the patch to the hull either with a rivet gun or a hammer and metal block.

NOTE:

If no mastic or bedding compound is available a watertight gasket can also be made from sailcloth, a towel, or a rag well greased or soaked in paint, primer, or asphalt.

Dents ■ 11

Small dents

These can be pounded out using a rubber mallet and a hard wood or metal block. Pounding should begin on the edge of the dent and move in concentric circles.

■ **11** *Method for reshaping a dent in aluminum*

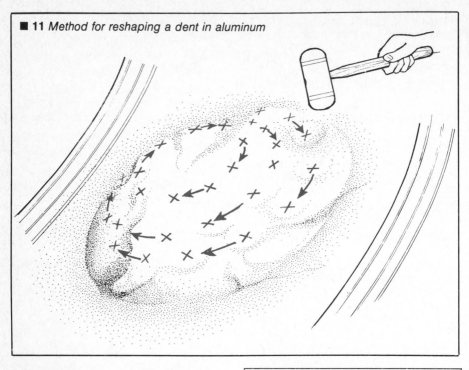

Larger dents

Those which may have stretched the metal often need a hole drilled in the center before they can be pounded back into shape. In this case, a patch must be riveted into place afterwards.

Alongside
See: Berthing

Anchoring

Anchoring signals

A vessel at anchor by day

A large black ball is hoisted into the rigging in the fore part of the vessel ■ **12**.

A vessel at anchor by night

Small boats – one white, all-round light visible two miles.

■ **12** *Daytime anchor signals*

■ **13** *Boats more than 165 feet (50 meters) in length*

Boats more than 165 feet (50 meters) in length – must also show an after light lower than the forward one ■ **13**.

Boats more than 330 feet (100 meters) in length – must also exhibit their deck lights ■ **14**.

Oil rigs

An all-round white light visible for ten miles and a red light at each corner visible for two miles ■ **15**.

All lights flash 'U' every 15 seconds.

■ **14** *Boats more than 330 feet (100 meters)*   ■ **15** *Oil rigs*

International Code of Signals

'Y'

YANKEE

'I AM DRAGGING MY ANCHOR!' ■ **16.**

For anchoring signals in fog or conditions of restricted visibility. **See: Fog**

Yellow
Red
Yellow
Red

■ 16

Anchoring principles

Type of bottom

Sand:	Plow or Danforth
Gravel:	Plow or Danforth

Mud:	Plow
A hard bottom:	Fisherman
Rocks:	Fisherman
Grass:	Plow or Fisherman

To identify the character of the bottom, consult a nautical chart, or use a hand lead armed with water pump grease, or **See: Echo sounders**

Scope

The ratio of anchor cable length to water depth should be:

Rope – Under favorable conditions 6:1
Under unfavorable conditions 8:1
Chain – Under favorable conditions 4:1
Under unfavorable conditions 5:1

Chain should make up at least a fathom or so of the anchor cable. This greatly increases holding power, acts as a shock absorber and prevents chafe on the bottom.

Windage

The wind's force on the boat rises with the square of the wind's speed. An anchor set, for example, in a 15-knot breeze will have twice the load when the wind speed is 22 knots, and nine times the load when the wind speed is 45 knots.

A windage alarm ■ 17

A length of cord or line is tied to the rode, and the other end to a deck fitting so that the line bears the strain on the anchor.

Several meters or a number of feet of rode are laid out on the deck.

When the wind increases, the line breaks and the loose rode runs out, bringing the yacht to with a jolt.

■ 17 *A windage alarm*

In a veering wind

Drop a second bow anchor underfoot in the direction toward which the wind is expected to veer ■ **18A**.

As the wind veers, and the boat swings, pay out the second anchor warp ■ **18B**, until the boat rides back safely on both anchors ■ **18C**.

NOTE:

In a crowded anchorage, anchor near boats using similar ground tackle, i.e., chain near chain, warp near warp. They will swing in the same manner as you do.

■ 18 *Anchoring in a veering wind*

Anchoring in strong tides or changing currents

METHOD 1 Anchors fore and aft

First drop the bow anchor upstream ■ **19A**.

Drift back to about double the length of the needed anchor cable, and dig in the anchor.

Drop the stern anchor ■ **19B**.

Pay out cable astern while winching or motoring upstream into position ■ **19C**.

For the length of the chain or warp required **See: A dragging anchor** (page 25)

■ **19** *Anchoring in tides and currents – Method 1*

WARNING:

If there is a lee-going ebb or flood, the strongest anchor should be set in the direction which will bear the most strain.

METHOD 2 Two bow anchors

First drop the bow anchor upstream ■ **20A**.

Drift back to about double the length of the needed anchor line.

Drop the second anchor ■ **20B**.

Winch or motor upstream, taking in the first anchor cable until in position.

Lead a rode through each bow chock to mooring cleats. Untwist rodes daily.

Lay out an additional 13–20ft. (4–6 m.) of warp, so that the keel will not foul the second anchor cable.

■ **20** *Anchoring in tides and currents – Method 2*

Anchoring in heavy weather or on a lee shore

METHOD 1 Backing the anchor ■ 21

Attach the kedge to a length of chain or rode and shackle or bend it to the main anchor ring.

Drop the kedge first, then while going astern release the main anchor.

NOTE:

Ideally, the kedge chain or rode should be slightly longer than the water depth, so that when retrieving the anchors one can be hoisted on board after the other.

■ 21 *Anchoring in heavy weather – Method 1*

METHOD 2 Double anchoring ■ 22

As in Method 1 – but drop the heavy anchor first and attach the heaviest remaining anchor 32 feet (10 meters) or more from it along the rode.

Do *not* drop both anchors at the same time.

This method should increase the holding power of the first anchor by about 100%.

Additional holding power can be added by sliding a weight down the chain. **See: A dragging anchor** (opposite)

WARNING:

1 – The Samson post or mooring cleat may need to be reinforced with a lashing to the mast.

■ 22 *Double anchoring – Method 2*

2 – If using chain, the bitter end should be secured in the chain locker with a lashing, in case the wind shifts and it is necessary to cut and run.

If the boat is yawing or lying at a difficult angle in relation to the water, this can be eased by

Leaving the main or mizzen hoisted and sheeted amidships.

Hanking a jib onto the backstay and sheeting it amidships.

Attaching a spring from the quarter to the anchor cable.

Steering the boat as if she were underway.

Lashing the helm in the best position.

A dragging anchor

To determine if the anchor is dragging, lower a lead line over the side until the weight touches bottom. Attach the end to a deck fitting and wait to see which way the line 'grows' ■ 23, 24. You may also simply observe two landmarks in range abeam.

■ **23** *Is the anchor dragging?*

■ **24** *Is the anchor dragging?*

The lead line can also be rigged as a 'frying pan' alarm ■ 25.

■ **25** *A 'frying pan' alarm*

If the anchor is dragging

Pay out more chain and/or rope.

Attach a weight – a piece of internal ballast, bucket of loose chain, or a string of shackles and rigging screws of at least 22 pounds (10 kilograms) – to the anchor warp with a large shackle. Then allow the weight to ride down the warp ■ 26, 27, 28.

The object is to make the pull on the anchor as nearly horizontal as possible.

The weight should be far enough along the line so that the bow will not be heavy.

■ **26** *A riding weight*

■ 27 *A riding weight*

■ 28 *A riding weight*

If the anchor continues to drag

Set a second anchor.

The angle between the two anchor lines should be about 30 degrees. This will provide *double* the holding power of a single anchor. However, as the angle increases, holding power decreases, until at an angle of 120 degrees between the anchor lines the holding power is the same as that of a single anchor laid out to windward.

Setting a second anchor under sail

Back the jib ■ **29A**.

Steer the boat as far as possible to one side ■ **29B**.

Drop the second anchor, then lie back on it.

■ 29 *Setting a second anchor under sail*

Setting a second anchor by dinghy

Lash the anchor securely over the dinghy's transom, keeping your feet clear of the rode ■ **30**.

Place the warp in the dinghy and pay it out gradually. The warp should be long enough to allow for the dinghy's drift. If necessary, a smaller line can be attached to the anchor warp, on the boat, then hauled in after the anchor is dropped.

A lone oarsman in a dink is ill-equipped to clear a snarl. If someone is available on the yacht, the warp can be flaked out on deck and payed out as needed.

Never row out chain. Instead, anchor the dinghy, and haul the chain to it on the warp. Then attach the chain to the anchor.

■ **30** *Setting an anchor by dinghy*

bit of chain over the anchor chain and, using a dinghy, tow it down until it reaches the anchor's crown. Then attempt to raise the anchor from the dinghy ■ **31**.

Anchoring the dinghy will help.

A fouled anchor

METHOD 1

Bring the bow directly over the anchor so that the rode is tight and vertical.

Secure the rode as short as possible with crew's weight in bow.

Move all hands aft, in order to use the boat's buoyancy to break the anchor out.

METHOD 2

Sail or motor over the anchor and attempt to pull it out from the other direction.

METHOD 3

Pass a ring, a large loop, or better still, a

■ **31** *Raising a fouled anchor*

METHOD 4

Using a line or chain approximately three times the length of the anchor rode, tow the loop as far down the rode as possible. Drop the dinghy's anchor, and when it is firmly dug in, attempt to break the boat's anchor free ■ **32**.

METHOD 5

If the anchor is fouled on another boat's chain

Attempt to raise *both* the anchor and the chain as high as possible.

Pass a line around the chain and secure it to the boat.

Free the anchor by hand or by dropping it.

Then release the chain ■ **33**.

METHOD 6

If the chain and anchor cannot be raised

A kedge or dinghy anchor will serve as a grapple.

Once the anchor is hooked, the line can either be pulled from different directions or taken back to the boat where the chain and anchor can be raised with a winch ■ **34**.

■ 32 *Raising a fouled anchor with a dinghy*

■ 34 *Dragging for a fouled anchor*

■ 33 *Raising a fouled anchor from on board*

A tripping line ■ 35

Many anchoring problems, particularly in new or unknown anchorages, can be prevented by attaching a *tripping line* to the anchor's crown. This line can be either buoyed or led back to the boat and secured to the anchor chain.

When buoyed, a short length of light chain

will hold the line straight in the water, making it less likely to be cut by a passing craft.

■ **35** *A tripping line*

chock to cockpit, drawing rode through chock as needed. Secure rode to mooring cleat allowing scope. When in position, drop anchor from cockpit.

A makeshift anchor ■ 37

Materials

Two sharpened pieces of hardwood.

A weight, such as a stone or piece of internal ballast.

Line or wire cable.

A makeshift plow ■ 38

Materials

A fisherman's anchor.

Line or wire.

A metal bucket.

Single-handed anchoring

Simple method

Before approaching anchorage, pass anchor outboard of all gear from bow

■ **36** *An anchor release for single-handers*

■ **37** *A makeshift anchor*

Antibiotics

After entering the body, antibiotics go to the area of infection and either kill the harmful bacteria or retard their growth so that the normal protection system of the body can function properly.

WARNING:

When taking antibiotics, do *not* drink alcohol.

■ 38

For chest, throat, and ear infections, boils, and infected cuts*

	Dosage
England and U.S.	
Tetracycline	500mg. 4 times/ day *for* 8 days
France	
Tetracycline	500mg. 4 times/ day *for* 8 days
Germany	
Doxycyclin	100mg. 2 times/ day *for* 8 days

If no improvement after 3–4 days, change to:

	Dosage
England and U.S.	
Ampicillin	500mg. 4 times/ day *for* 8 days
France	
Totapen	500mg. 4 times/ day *for* 8 days

	Dosage
Germany	
Binotal	500mg. 4 times/ day *for* 8 days

WARNING:

If allergic to penicillin, do *not* take ampicillin. Take erythromycin instead in the same dosage twice a day.

*** NOTE:**

For infected cuts, take *only* tetracyline.

NOTE:

Oral antibiotics often irritate the gastrointestinal tract, and may cause nausea, vomiting and diarrhea.

For urinary-tract infections

	Dosage
England	
Septrin	2 tablets 2 times/ day
France and U.S.	
Bactrim	2 tablets 2 times/ day

	Dosage
Germany	
Bactrim	2 tablets 2 times/ day

For dysentery

	Dosage
England and U.S.	
Tetracycline	500mg. 4 times/ day *for* 10 days
France	
Tetracycline	500mg. 4 times/ day *for* 10 days
Germany	
Doxycyclin	100mg. 2 times/ day *for* 10 days

If no improvement after
3–4 days, take:

	Dosage
England	
Flagyl	800mg. 3 times/ day *for* 10 days
France	
Flagyl	800mg. 3 times/ day *for* 10 days
Germany	
Flagyl	800mg. 3 times/ day *for* 10 days

	Dosage
U.S.	
Flagyl	500– 750mg. 3 times/ day *for* 10 days

NOTE:

Do *not* drink alcohol while taking Flagyl.

For skin infection and minor infected wounds

Before applying topical antibiotics wash the area with warm, soapy water and antiseptic. **See: Antiseptics**

Topical antibiotics

	Dosage
England	
Neomycin	5mg. Apply 2–4 times/day
Bacitracin zinc	500 units/ gram Apply 2–4 times/day
France	
Neomycin	5mg. Apply 2–4 times/day
Bacitracin zinc	500 units/ gram Apply 2–4 times/day
Germany	
Neomycin	5mg. Apply 2–4 times/day

Dosage

Nebacitin ointment
  Apply 2–4
  times/day

U.S.
Bacitracin ointment
  Apply 2–4
  times/day
Neosporin ointment
  Apply 2–4
  times/day

For eye infections (conjunctivitis)

Dosage

England and U.S.
Chloramphenicol   A small
ointment or drops amount of
                   ointment
                   or 2 drops
                   to affected
                   eye every
                   3–6 hours

France
Collyre
Chloramphénicol

Germany
Paraxin Augensalbe

WARNING:

When taking antibiotics, do *not* drink alcohol.

Antiseptics

See also: Sterilization

Antiseptics are chemical agents which *inhibit* the growth and development of microorganisms, but do not necessarily kill them. Disinfectants kill bacteria.

Antiseptics

England and U.S.

Hydrogen peroxide
Mercurochrome
Alcohol

France

Eau oxygenée
Mercurochrome
Alcohol

Germany

Wasserstoff peroxid
Mercurochrom
Alkohol

NOTE:

In emergencies, such as on liferafts, urine may be used.

Disinfectants

England and U.S.

Tincture of iodine
Diluted bleach, 1 teaspoon per quart or liter

France

Teinture d'iode
Eau de javel diluée, 1 teaspoon per quart or liter

Germany

Merfen*
Bleichlauge, 1 teaspoon per quart or liter

Tincture of iodine is not sold in Germany.

Appendicitis

Symptoms

A dull pain* which begins in the central

abdomen, and after a few hours moves to the lower right-hand quarter, becoming localized, sharper, more severe, and causing spasms of the overlying muscles.

Vomiting may occur.

The breath is foul.

Later, the stomach wall becomes hard and tender to the touch.

A moderate fever.

*NOTE:

Other possible causes of a dull pain

Food poisoning: pain is less well defined and accompanied by more vomiting and diarrhea.

Constipation: Pain is sharp, comes and goes and produces no muscle spasms or fever.

Swollen abdominal glands: pain is less precise, and without muscle spasms. Usually occurs in younger people following a sore throat.

Treatment for appendicitis

The *only* certain treatment is surgery.

Until then, the person should be put to bed, given no food or purgatives, but allowed occasional sips of water.

Administer *only* a 'moderate' painkiller. A narcotic will tend to cause intestinal spasms. **See: Pain killers**

If a fever and malaise develop, take ampicillin. **See: Antibiotics**

Peritonitis, that is, inflammation of the intestinal wall, rarely occurs within eight hours of the onset of appendicitis, but if untreated by surgery is fatal.

Explanation

Appendicitis is an inflammation of a blind sac which leads from the beginning of the large intestine. The difficulty in recognizing it is that the position of the sac may vary, thereby changing the site of the pain.

Artificial respiration

If the person is not breathing

Begin mouth-to-mouth resuscitation *at once* ■ 39.

Tilt the head backwards, press down on the forehead, and push the lower jaw upwards by pressing the jawbone below the ear.

Clear the mouth and throat of any foreign matter.

Seal your lips around the person's mouth, hold his nose closed with your fingers and forceably blow air into his mouth.

After each breath remove your mouth in order to allow the person to breathe out normally.

Inflate the lungs 3–5 times, then watch for chest movement.

If the air passages are not clear

Roll the person on his side and deliver a sharp blow between the shoulder blades.

Maintain a steady rhythm of 10–12 breaths per minute.

If there is no movement of the person's chest

and

His color is deathly blue-gray.

The pupils of his eyes are dilated.

No pulse can be felt.

The heart has stopped.

Immediately try to revive the heart

Turn the person on his back.

Hit the chest smartly over the lower part of the breast bone.

If the heart does not begin to beat

Kneel beside the person; *begin cardiopulmonary resuscitation.*

Place the heel of one hand on the lower
end of the breast bone, the other hand on
top of it, and press down firmly and evenly
by rocking forward with your arms
straight.

For adults – once a second.
Children – 80 times a minute.
Babies – 100 times a minute.

Avoid a jerky action.

If alone

Alternate mouth-to-mouth resuscitation
with cardiopulmonary resuscitation – one
deep inflation of the lungs, then five heart
compressions.

■ **39** *Mouth-to-mouth resuscitation: inflate, and allow to deflate*

If two people

One person does the mouth-to-mouth
resuscitation, the other the
cardiopulmonary resuscitation with a
rhythm of one inflation to five heart
compressions.

B

Backstay

See: Rigging failures

Baggywrinkle

See also: Chafe, Sail repair

Materials

For 3ft. (1 meter) of baggywrinkle – about 10ft. (3 meters) of 1½in. (3.5–4cm.) old rope.

Two lengths of marline.

Procedure

Unlay the rope and cut it into 4in. (10cm.) strands.

Tie two lengths of marline in a vertical position between two fittings.

Take a strand of rope, hold it crosswise, bring the ends up outside the twine, then pass them inside ■ 40.

Slide the strand up firmly against the knot.

Take the next strand . . . and so on.

Press the strands tightly against each other and knot the twine to hold them in place.

Unhitch the twine ■ 41.

Tape the sections of shroud where the baggywrinkle is lashed so it will not slip down ■ 42.

NOTE:

Instant baggywrinkle can be fabricated from paint rollers or smooth plastic pipe.

■ 40 *Baggywrinkle*   ■ 41 *Baggywrinkle*   ■ 42 *Baggywrinkle*

Bare poles	Beaching
See: Running	See: Aground

Barometer	Beacons
See: Weather forecast	See: Lights

Beaufort wind scale

(Beaufort nbr.−1)×5=knots per hr. Use this formula to make a rough conversion from Beaufort number to wind velocity in knots per hour:

DETERMINATION OF WIND SPEED BY SEA CONDITION

Knots	Descriptive	Sea Conditions	Wind force (Beaufort)	Probable wave height (in ft.)
0–1	Calm	Sea smooth and mirror-like.	0	–
1–3	Light air	Scale-like ripples without foam crests.	1	¼
4–6	Light breeze	Small, short wavelets; crests have a glassy appearance and do not break.	2	½
7–10	Gentle breeze	Large wavelets; some crests begin to break; foam of glassy appearance. Occasional white foam crests.	3	2
11–16	Moderate breeze	Small waves, becoming longer; fairly frequent white foam crests.	4	4
17–21	Fresh breeze	Moderate waves, taking a more pronounced long form; many white foam crests; there may be some spray.	5	6
22–27	Strong breeze	Large waves begin to form; white foam crests are more extensive everywhere; there may be some spray.	6	10
28–33	Near gale	Sea heaps up and white foam from breaking waves begins to be blown in streaks along the direction of the wind; spindrift begins.	7	14
34–40	Gale	Moderately high waves of greater length; edges of crests break into spindrift; foam is blown in well-marked streaks along the direction of the wind.	8	18
41–47	Strong gale	High waves; dense streaks of foam along the direction of the wind; crests of waves begin to topple, tumble, and roll over; spray may reduce visibility.	9	23
48–55	Storm	Very high waves with long overhanging crests. The resulting foam in great patches is blown in dense white streaks along the direction of the wind. On the whole, the surface of the sea is white in appearance. The tumbling of the sea becomes heavy and shock-like. Visibility is reduced.	10	29
56–63	Violent Storm	Exceptionally high waves that may obscure small and medium-sized ships. The sea is completely covered with long white patches of foam lying along the direction of the wind. Everywhere the edges of the wave crests are blown into froth. Visibility reduced.	11	37
64–71	Hurricane	The air is filled with foam and spray. Sea completely white with driving spray; visibility very much reduced.	12	45

(Courtesy National Weather Service)

Berthing (Coming Alongside)

Alongside pilings and uneven walls

Rig a fenderboard, or an old plank can be tied across two or more fenders ■ **43.**
See: Fenders

The fenders can be strung on a line horizontally like sausages ■ **44.**

Three or more fenders can be tied together to form a fat one ■ **45.**

■ **43** *Berthing alongside uneven walls*

■ **44**

■ **45**

Alongside, without touching the dock

Tie up on the downwind, downstream side of the dock, if possible.

A kedge anchor can be laid out abeam.

If the boat is moored with springs, the warp can be attached at bow or stern ■ **46.**

The warp can also be passed under the keel to the other side, giving the kedge more scope and holding power. ■ **47.**
See: Careening

■ **46** *Alongside, without touching the dock*

■ **47** *Alongside, without touching the dock*

WARNING:

Use chafing gear along the toe rail. **See: Chafe**

Also beware of chafe against the keel ■ **48**.

■ **48** *Alongside, without touching the dock*

Stern-to (common in Europe)

Instead of dropping anchor and maneuvering in reverse

Approach the dock bow-on ■ **49A**.

Attach a line from the bow to the dock ■ **49B**.

Back the boat out ■ **49C**.

Turn, then drop an anchor from the bow. Pass the warp attached to the dock to the stern ■ **49D**.

While paying out the anchor cable, warp the boat into her berth at the dock.

■ **49** *Berthing stern-to*

Bilge pump

See: Holes

Bleeding

See: Hemorrhages

Birds

See: Landfall signs, Liferaft

Block and tackle

■ **50** *Single whip: 1:1* ■ **51** *Runner: 2:1* ■ **52** *Double whip: 2:1* ■ **53** *Jigger: 3:1* ■ **54** *Handy billy: 4:1*

Booms

See also: Dismasted, Rigging failures

Broken

METHOD 1

Oars, floorboards, or boathooks can be used as splints, and the two broken pieces lashed together.

METHOD 2

The boom can be removed entirely and the mainsail set loose footed, but since the sail is no longer bent to the boom, more than likely the clew will need to be reinforced. **See: Sail repair**

Mainsails with reef points

Remove the boom and reef the sail until the foot is about the same length as an oar, jib boom, or spinnaker pole.

Loosely tie one end of the pole to the mast ■ **55A**.

Then, *either* lash the sail to the pole through the reef points ■ **55B** *or* tie it to the pole with the reefing line ■ **55C**.

Attach the mainsheet directly to the end of the jury-rigged boom. ■ **55D** The advantage of this method is that it removes strain from the mainsail clew.

■ **55** *Jury-rigging a boom for a mainsail with reef points*

Bosun's chair

See: Climbing the mast

Bowline

See also: Knots

One-handed

■ **56** *Tying a one-handed bowline*

A

B

C

D

With your *left hand*, grasp the long end firmly to hold the tension.

Pass the short end around you ■ **56A**.

Take the tip of the short end in your *right hand* and bring it up to the slack portion of the line ■ **56B**.

Grasp the slack and twist it into a loop so that the tip of the short end passes through it ■ **56C**.

Pull a bit of line through the loop ■ **56D**, then pass it underneath the slack ahead of the loop ■ **56E**.

Pull the line back through the loop and tighten the knot ■ **56F**.

NOTE:

A man's life may depend on his ability to tie this knot quickly in the dark.

E

F

Broaching to

See: Heavy weather

Broken bones

See: Fractures

Bulldog clamps (wire rope clips)

See also: Dismasting, Rigging failures

Procedure

Wire rope clips should be used in groups of 3 ■ **57**.

One clip should be placed close to the eye ■ **57A**.

The two other clips can be spaced 2–3in. (5–6cm.) apart ■ **57B**.

The block of the clip must be against the standing part of the rigging, or the longer section of wire ■ **57C**. This will ensure a strength of approximately 85–90% of that of the wire. If the clips are placed the wrong way around the strength drops to about 75%.

Burns

Treatment

For minor burns

Leave the wound open.

Or coat completely with:
Plastic skin.
Plain soap dissolved in a little water.
A paste of bicarbonate of soda and water.

To lessen pain and help prevent blisters, immediately soak the wound in cold or iced water for 15–30 minutes.

NOTE:

If possible, do *not* break blisters as they

■ **57** *Wire rope clips*

are a natural sterile covering until new skin forms underneath. If blisters must be broken, do so along the edge with a sterile needle, and then wash the wound with antiseptic or antiseptic cream. **See: Antiseptic.** Do *not* remove the blistered skin.

For major burns (more than 10% of the body)

Cleanse the burned areas thoroughly with soap and water.

Do *not* put on oils, salves or ointments.

Leave the wound open.

Victim should be kept warm.

Give the victim plenty of warm, salty fluids – for example: a mixture of $\frac{1}{2}$ teaspoon salt, $\frac{1}{2}$ teaspoon bicarbonate of soda, and 1 quart or liter of water and orange juice – for palatability and potassium.

See: Pain killers, Shock

Rope burns

If the skin is *not* broken – pour cold water over the area for 5–10 minutes. Do not cover it.

If the skin is broken, cover with a nonadhesive dressing.

Burned mouth

Suck on a piece of ice, or wash the mouth with cold water.

The pain of a burned mouth can often be lessened by slowly drinking some cream or by sucking on some butter.

C

Cardiopulmonary resuscitation

See: Artificial respiration

Careening

Light displacement craft can usually be heeled over to expose nearly their entire keel, heavier craft to within a foot or two of the keel. For this reason careening is an excellent technique for:

Emergency hull repair.

Rudder repairs.

Seacock repairs.

Changing anodes.

Cleaning and painting the bottom.

METHOD 1   Careening from off the dock ■ 58

Prerequisites

A dock and calm water.

Strong anchors and chain.

Chafing gear. **See: Chafe**

A strong block and tackle of at least 4 to 1. **See: Block and tackle**

Procedure

Remove as much weight as possible from the boat. To lessen the strain on the mast, shift internal ballast to the side nearest the dock.

Also remove such items as batteries, which could be damaged when the boat is heeled over.

Close all seacocks, portholes, cockpit lockers, sink drains and companionways.

Seal the fuel tanks to prevent overflow.

Move the boat off the dock to a distance about ¾ the height of the mast.

Moor the boat fore and aft.

Lay out an anchor – or two – abeam, allowing plenty of scope. Pass the cable under the keel, secure it with chafing gear amidships, then lash it round the mast.

Pass a strop around the mast, supported by the halyard. Clap a block and tackle to the strop and hoist it by the halyard to the lower spreader. Take a strain on the block and tackle, taking care that the spreader is not damaged as the yacht heels.

Slowly heel the boat over.

WARNING:

When heeled over, wooden boats may tend to leak through their topsides if they have not been sailed frequently.

■ 58 *Careening from off the dock*

METHOD 2   Careening alongside the dock ■ 59

Prerequisites

A dock and calm weather

At least 5 car tires

A large strong plank

A heavy car or truck

Procedure

Slacken the boat's mooring lines, fore and aft.

Lash the car tires together, and secure them to the dock so that they hang into the water.

Secure the plank in place between the hull and the tires.

Take a heavy warp, pass a bight around the mast, then hoist it to the spreader with the main halyard. Tie the other end to a strong point on the car or truck.

While heeling the boat slowly, watch the rigging and lifelines in order that they do not come in contact with the quay.

NOTE:

For light displacement boats it may be possible to lash securely the fall of the main halyard and carry the other end directly to the car. A wire halyard will be seriously damaged if used in this way. Use it as a messenger to reeve a warp before taking a strain.

■ **59** *Careening alongside the dock*

Cardiac arrest

See: Artificial respiration

Chafe

On lines at dockside

Cover the bights with plastic hose. Slitting the plastic hose down one side allows easy installation ■ 60.

Wind lengths of old rope around them ■ 61.

For quick protection, bind the rope with old rags ■ 62.

Use bights of chain.

For protection of a bight slide a length of plastic tubing over the rope, then splice in an eye. A second piece of hose or tubing can be added and left so that it can be adjusted ■ 63. Old hose which is rigid is often preferable. It will hold the bight open, allowing mooring lines to be thrown easily over pilings or bollards.

Protection against chafe

■ **60**   ■ **61**   ■ **62**

If the chafed line must pass through a block

Cut a length of light canvas into strips 1–1¼in. (2–3cm.) wide.

Wrap them around the line against the lay and secure them in place with twine, following the lay of the line. If tightly bound, this will only slightly increase the diameter ■ **64**.

If a line, passing through a block, is in danger of being chafed

Make a series of whippings covering the area of possible chafe.

■ **63** *Protection of a bight*

■ **64** *Chafe protection*

To prevent a tangle in case chafe occurs

Make short whippings every 4in. (10cm.) ■ **65**.

An advantage of this method is that, should the line chafe through, it will not jam the block.

■ **65** *Jam-free chafe protection*

If the line is badly chafed

Short splice ■ 66

Cut the line and rejoin the ends with a short splice. This will restore about 95% of the original strength.

Long splice ■ 67

Cut the line and rejoin the ends with a long splice. This will restore 60% of the original strength, but its advantage is that the line's diameter is only slightly increased, hence it will pass through a block.

Whipping ■ 68

Cut the line. Tightly whip each end, then sew them together with strong twine and bind the whippings. This method should not be used for load-bearing lines.

■ **66** *Short splice*

■ **67** *Long splice*

NOTE:

Whipping is the only way to re-reeve halyards (using messengers) without going aloft, as when end-for-ending on internal halyards.

■ **68** *Joining lines by whippings*

Sheetbend ■ 69

■ **69** *Joining lines by a sheetbend*

■ **70** *Joining lines with two bowlines*

Bowline ■ 70

Cut the line, and rejoin the ends using two bowlines. This will restore about 50% of the original strength, so should not be used for load-bearing lines.

For chafe on sails

Slide a split plastic hose up the after lower shrouds.

See also: Baggywrinkle, Sail Repair

Climbing the mast

When climbing the mast without a bosun's chair

If you have help, wear a safety harness attached to a halyard so that your helper can keep a strain on it in case you slip.

Remain fully dressed.

Wear full-fingered gloves when ascending or descending, but not woolen ones, as they tend to slip.

Wear sea boots, as they will grip the mast more firmly than shoes.

At night

Tape a flashlight to your forearm, so you have two hands free.

In heavy weather

Do *not* heave to. If possible, sail with the wind abeam. When aloft, roll is easier to cope with than pitch.

Secure a downhaul to the bosun's chair.

Wear a lifejacket for protection in case you swing into the mast.

Attach a short length of line and a snap hook to the chair to secure yourself aloft.

If no bosun's chair is on board, one may be improvised from:

A tubular fender ■ **71.**

A boarding ladder ■ **72.**

A bowline on the bight ■ **73.**

Climbing alone with sliding stirrups

Make mast-encircling stirrups from two lengths of line about 6ft. (3m.) long. Tie a bowline for your foot in one end. Tie the other end snugly around the mast sheet high while standing in the stirrup. Tie the end of the other stirrup around the mast as high as you can reach when your foot is loosely in its stirrup. The loops around the mast should be loose enough to slide up but tight enough not to slide down when you put your full weight in its stirrup. Alternately put your weight on one, then reach down and slide the loop of the other up the mast and stand up in it, reach down again and slide the other up, put your weight in it.

■ **74** *Climbing alone with sliding stirrups*

Emergency bosun's chair

■ **71**

■ **72**

■ **73**

To make a ladder

METHOD 1 ■ 75, 76

Lay a length of stiff rope, such as a warp, on the deck, and at 1ft. (¹/₃m.) intervals, tie large overhand knots to form stirrup-like bights.

Hoist the chain of loops aloft on a halyard, twist it several times around the mast to prevent it from swinging, then secure it tightly to a pin or cleat.

NOTE:

If the ladder is not long enough, the climber can secure himself to the crosstrees. The ladder can be unwound, hoisted to the masthead, then respiraled for the next stage of the climb.

METHOD 2 ■ 77

Lay a length of line on the deck – about three times the height of the ladder required – double it, then tie sheepshanks to form the steps.

Hoist the ladder aloft on a halyard and secure the end to the base of the mast.

■ 75 ■ 76 *A rope ladder from overhand knots*

■ 77 *A rope ladder from sheepshanks*

METHOD 3 ■ 78

Using lengths of heavy cord, attach temporary ratlines to the shrouds with stopper knots (rolling hitches). **See: Knots**

With a little practice, these knots can be tied with one hand, leaving the other free to hang on with. If the lengths of cord are precut, they can be tied in place, one by one, as an ascent is made.

On an average-sized yacht, 8–12 lines should be enough to reach the crosstrees. Above that, if necessary, a web of ratlines can be tied between the upper shrouds, the mast and/or the forestay.

NOTE:

If the knots are being tied on stainless steel wire, a few turns of tape just below each knot will help it gain purchase.

METHOD 4 ■ 79

You should carry a few lengths of oak in the bilge anyway for splinting broken spars. Cut rungs tied with marlin spike hitches between two spare sheets to form a Jacob's ladder.

The ladder is tied to the main halyard, hoisted aloft, then cleated securely to the base of the mast.

METHOD 5 ■ 80

If the sail slides and their lashings are sufficiently strong, the mainsail can be slightly lowered and the slack in the sail used as ladder steps.

For single-handers

Make it a point to carry a light anchor rode five times the mast height above deck.

■ **78** *Ratlines*   ■ **79** *Jacob's ladder*   ■ **80** *Climbing the sail*

Make up a long block and tackle – two or three lines. **See: Block and tackle**

To go to the spreaders with a mechanical advantage of 4:1 you will need at least four times the height.

Rig tackle so hauling part leads down to chair from upper end, and mechanical advantage will include hauling part.

Hoist one end of the block and tackle to the masthead or spreaders. Since the lines tend to twist, and friction eats up the advantage, this method works best if there is a swivel at the upper block. The twist varies with the weight on the chair. Before sitting down, untwist the tackle under strain while holding it down with one foot; the tackle will render easily.

Attach the other end of the block and tackle to a bosun's chair, and haul yourself aloft.

Clouds

See: Weather forecast

Coach-roof repair

See: Deckhouse repair

Collision

See also: Accidents

■ **81** *Climbing the mast*

If you think you are on a collision course with another vessel

Take an accurate bearing.

Wait, then take another bearing.

If the bearing remains constant, *you are on a collision course!*

■ **82** *The angles remain equal, but the triangle grows smaller*

Avoiding action

Make all maneuvers boldly and decisively so that the other ship will clearly understand your intentions.

If you suspect the other vessel has not seen you:

By day

Sound the appropriate warning signal of five or more short blasts on the horn.

By night

Flash the appropriate warning signal of five flashes or a morse 'U'.

or

Shine a strong torch up to the sails or let off a white flare.

NOTE:

A white flare does *not* indicate distress.
See: Flares

If there is a choice between changing course and changing speed, *change course.*

When changing course

Make the change a large one.

Change from one fixed course to another fixed course.

It is always safer to pass astern of another vessel.

If under sail, one must give way to

Sailing vessels on the starboard tack.

Other sailing boats which are on the same tack to leeward.

Other sailing boats which are running free.

A vessel engaged in fishing.

A vessel navigating in a Traffic Separation Lane.

A vessel hampered by her draft such as a bulk carrier or supertanker.

A vessel restricted in her ability to maneuver such as a dredger or vessel laying a buoy.

A vessel not under command.

If under power one must also give way to

A vessel under sail unless being overtaken.

A vessel on the starboard side forward of the beam.

WARNING:

When avoiding fishing boats try to allow at least 500ft. (150 meters) for their nets.

NOTE:

If there is a risk of a *head-on collision*, both vessels alter course to starboard.

If a collision is inevitable

Attempt to turn onto the same course as the other vessel.

Attempt not to be struck directly abeam.

If you have the right of way, and the other vessel is to port, turn to starboard if possible.

Warning signals

NOTE:

If the signals are made by light, the *duration* of each flash should be about *one second*, the *interval* between flashes about *one second*, and the *interval between signals* at least *10 seconds*.

If the signals are made by sound, the *duration* of each short blast should be about *one second*, a long blast, *4–6 seconds*.

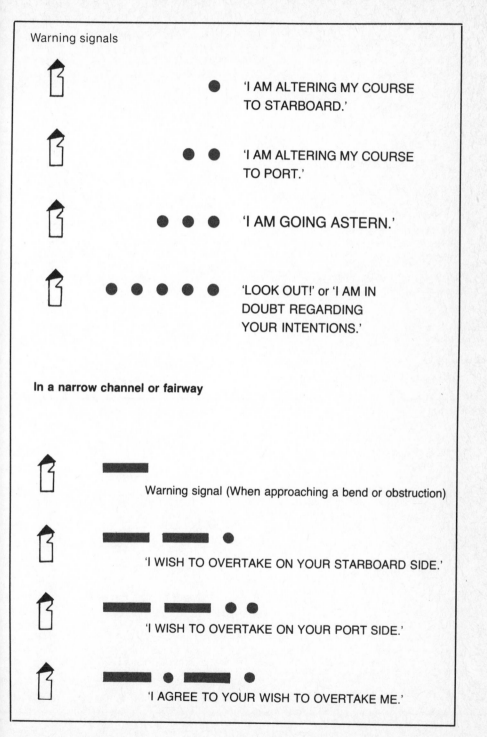

Warning signals

'I AM ALTERING MY COURSE TO STARBOARD.'

'I AM ALTERING MY COURSE TO PORT.'

'I AM GOING ASTERN.'

'LOOK OUT!' or 'I AM IN DOUBT REGARDING YOUR INTENTIONS.'

In a narrow channel or fairway

Warning signal (When approaching a bend or obstruction)

'I WISH TO OVERTAKE ON YOUR STARBOARD SIDE.'

'I WISH TO OVERTAKE ON YOUR PORT SIDE.'

'I AGREE TO YOUR WISH TO OVERTAKE ME.'

Collision mat

See: Holes

Constipation

Treatment

Plenty of fluids – preferably hot – fresh fruit, vegetables, and exercise should provide the solution.

If not:

Mild laxatives are: bran, garlic, wheat germ, brown rice, raisins and other dried fruits.

Strong laxatives are: boiled coffee, Epsom salts, three tablespoons of either olive or corn oil.

Explanation

Constipation is usually caused by a change in diet or environment, hence it often accompanies the beginning of a voyage. When the body adjusts to a new routine, regularity usually returns. Two or three days without a bowel movement will not do the body any harm. The record is over 100 days!

Medication

	Dosage
U.S. and Europe	
Dulcolax*	10mg.

*Will require 6–12 hours for evacuation. If possible, take before going to bed.

For chronic constipation: Take an enema of one quart (or one liter) tepid fresh water.

Cyclones

See: Law of storms

D

Danger

International Code of Signals

'U'

UNIFORM

'YOU ARE RUNNING INTO DANGER!'

Red   White

■ 83 ● ● ▬▬▬▬

'PS' (Often used by light vessels)

'YOU SHOULD NOT COME ANY CLOSER.'

■ 84

Damage control gear

See: Holes

Date

If the date is unknown

Nearly all radio stations broadcast the date at either midnight or 0100 hours.

NOTE:

Should the announcement be in a foreign language, it is often easier to record the broadcast on a tape recorder, and decipher it later. For the numbers in eight languages, **See: Numbers**

The date by moon sight

Prerequisites

A sextant.

The Nautical Almanac.

The time (GMT)

Sight Reduction Tables.

Your approximate position, *plus or minus* one degree of latitude and/or longitude.

The approximate date, *plus or minus* 2–3 days.

Principle

The moon's place in the heavens changes dramatically from one day to the next, often passing through 12 degrees of

Hour Angle (celestial longitude) and several degrees of Declination (celestial latitude) in 24 hours. The sun, by contrast, changes its Hour Angle and Declination gradually, only a few minutes a day. Hence a moon sight calculated with the Hour Angle and Declination of the *wrong date* will yield an imposssible position line, one that is hundreds of miles from your approximate position. The position closest to your estimated position is the one with the correct date.

Procedure

Take a moon sight during either the day or night.

Using the Hour Angle and Declination of three or four consecutive days, work out the position lines in the usual manner. It will *not* be necessary to make the 'v' and 'd' corrections, as rough calculations will be sufficient.

Plot all the lines and label them by date.

All but one should be impossible. If not, or in doubt, wait until the moon is in another quadrant and repeat the process.

Death

Signs of death

No pulse or heartbeat.

The pupils of the eyes are fixed and dilated.

No reaction to painful stimuli, for example, when jabbed with a pin or needle.

No fogging of a mirror held close to the nostrils or mouth.

Decreased body temperature.

Blue marks on those parts of the body on which the dead person has been lying.

After 2–3 hours joints become difficult to move.

Deckhouse repair

Storm or wave damage

For cracks, broken deck joints and plank separations, the area to be reinforced is at deck level.

Shoring can be cut from dinghy oars, spars, or boathooks.

Padding can be cut from floorboards, locker doors, or bulkheads.

Wedges can be cut from paint brush handles, cutting boards, or tools – such as chisels, screwdrivers, etc.

■ **85** *Reinforcing a weakened deckhouse*

Demasted

See: Dismasted

Diarrhea

Treatment

No food for 24 hours.

If the person is not vomiting, sufficient

liquids to prevent dehydration, for example, boiled skimmed milk, tea, bouillon, or clear broths.

No alcohol or coffee.

Only 'mild' medication for the first 24 hours.

If diarrhea continues, or is severe, stronger medication should be considered.

Medication

Mild: cooked, unseasoned white rice, carrot soup, yogurt, crushed bananas, cheese, apple juice and apple sauce.

Strong:

	Dosage
England and U.S. Lomotil	1–2 tablets/ 4hrs.
North America Kaopectate	4–8 tablespoons
France Diarsed	1–2 tablets/ 4hrs.
Germany Imodium	2 tablets/ 6hrs.

Complications

Diarrhea can signal the beginning of a serious illness, such as typhoid fever or dysentery, **See: Antibiotics,** hence the patient should be watched carefully.

Diarrhea can be even more dangerous to small children as they can become dehydrated more quickly than adults.

Explanation

The two common causes of diarrhea are:

1 – Consuming bad food or drink, such as unripe or overripe fruit, bad tinned foods, inferior wine or beer, or impure water.

2 – Food contaminated by bacteria, such as that badly cleaned or prepared, kept too long, or left in reach of flies or other insects.

If the cause has been unwholesome food or drink, the symptoms should lessen noticeably after six hours.

Diesel engine

See: Engine failure – diesel

Disabled

See also: Distress signals

International Code of Signals

'**D**'   DELTA

'KEEP CLEAR OF ME; I AM MANEUVERING WITH DIFFICULTY!'

Yellow

Blue

■ 86

'**F**'   FOXTROT

'I AM DISABLED; COMMUNICATE WITH ME!'

White

Red

■ 87

Dismasted

See also: Jury-rigging, Rigging failures

If the mast, or any part of it goes overboard, the **immediate danger** *is*

The mast will stave in the hull.

or

The tangled rigging and sail will act as a sea anchor and drag the weather rail into the water.

Depending on sea and weather conditions

Hoist the broken mast on board.

Bring the mast alongside and lash it to the hull.

Salvage boom, sail, and rigging.

Tow the mast at a safe distance from the boat.

Lie to it as a sea anchor from the bow or stern.

Clear the deck

First, attempt to open the turnbuckles or remove the clevis pins.

Cut through any bronze turnbuckles as they are softer than rigging wire.

Cut through galvanized wire stays with shears, croppers, abrasive wheel, hacksaw, or hammer and cold chisel against a metal block.

See: Rigging failures

Cut the stainless steel wire with bolt cutters or a hammer and cold chisel against a metal block.

If the broken mast cannot be hoisted on board by hand

METHOD 1 ■ 88

A line is run through a block on the mast stump and then to the halyard winch.

■ **88** *Hoisting the mast on board with the mast stump*

METHOD 2 ■ 89

A spinnaker pole or jib boom is lashed to the mast and braced by a stanchion to serve as a crane arm.

■ **89** *Hoisting the mast on board with the spinnaker pole*

METHOD 3 ■ 90

If the boat has two masts, the mizzen boom is run out abeam and used as a crane arm.

■ **90** *Hoisting the mast on board with the mizzen*

If the mast cannot be hoisted on board

It should be lashed alongside, well out of the water.

Put out all fenders. For emergency fenders **See: Fenders**

Run a line from the mast, through a block on the bow pulpit to the cockpit winch and raise the mast out of the water.

Lash the mast tightly to the hull using as many lines as possible ■ **91**.

WARNING:

If the mast or fittings endanger the hull, they should be cut away.

■ **91** *Lashing the mast alongside*

If the mast cannot be brought alongside

It must be towed at a safe distance from the boat ■ **92**.

For towing gear **See: Towing**

■ **92** *Towing a broken mast*

If only the upper section of the mast is broken, but still on board

Do not try to cut off the downcoming part.

Secure it from the masthead to the stayed portion of the mast or a deck fitting ■ **93**.

A block and tackle will probably be necessary ■ **94**.

If the lower portion of the mast is bent or broken, but still on board

Lash the two sections together ■ **93**.

Lash the broken piece to another part of the boat so that the two portions of the mast become a strong triangle ■ **95**.

Securing a broken mast

■ **93**   ■ **94**   ■ **95**

Distance at sea

For a person on deck, about 7ft. (2 meters) above the water

A rough guide is:

Distance – 4 miles

To shore
Objects, such as trees and houses are recognizable, but only in form. The beach is not visible.

To ships at sea
The superstructure of large ships can be seen. A yacht is a white spot.

Distance – 3 miles

To shore
Roofs and chimneys can be determined. Heavy surf can be seen.

To ships at sea
Freighter markings and bow waves are visible.

Distance – 2 miles

To shore
Windows and doors can be distinguished. But people are still invisible.

To ships at sea
Large buoys are barely discernible. At night, ship's sidelights come into view.

Distance – 1 mile

To shore
Details appear on buildings. Traffic can be seen and people are dots.

To ships at sea
Smaller buoys become visible, and freighter portholes.

Distance – ½ mile

To shore
People are moving lines, cars are identifiable.

To ships at sea
Sailors can be seen on deck. Rigging can be discerned.

Distance-off

METHOD 1   Vertical Sextant Angle ■ 96

Sight an object on shore, such as a lighthouse, whose height is known or can be estimated, and measure its angle above sea level. No allowance need be made for the height of the eye above the water (the dip) or the state of the tide, as the result is an approximation.

Select the column in the table which is closest to the height of the object. Read down to find your Sextant Angle, interpolate if necessary, then read off the distance on the vertical scale.

NOTE:

The heights of lighthouses are given to the center of their lanterns, not to the top of their structures.

Distance-off in miles	*Height of the object ashore in meters (and feet)*				
	12 (40ft.)	15 (50ft.)	21 (70ft.)	30 (100ft.)	40 (135ft.)
½	45′	57′	1° 19′	1° 53′	2° 27′
1	23′	28′	40′	57′	1° 14′
2	11′	14′	20′	28′	37′
3	8′	9′	13′	19′	24′
4	—	—	10′	14′	18′
5	—	—	—	11′	15′

■ 96 *Measuring the distance-off by a vertical Sextant Angle*

METHOD 2   A Bow-and-Beam (45°) Bearing ■ 97

Take a bearing on any stationary object which is 45 degrees off the bow.

With a log or speedometer, measure the distance between that point, A, and a second one, B, when the object, C, is directly abeam at 90 degrees.

Make allowances for tide and current.

At that moment the two sides of the triangle are equal, AB=BC. The distance traveled from point A to point B equals the distance from point B to the object at C.

METHOD 3   Doubling the angle on the bow ■ 98

Take a bearing from point A to any stationary object, C, which is *more than* 20 degrees off the bow.

With a log or speedometer measure the distance between that point, A, and a second one, B, when the angle off the bow is exactly double.

Make allowances for tide and current.

At that moment the two sides of the triangle are equal, AB=BC, but *not* necessarily joined by a right angle. The distance traveled from A to B then equals the distance from B to the object at C.

■ **97** *Distance-off by a bow-and-beam bearing*

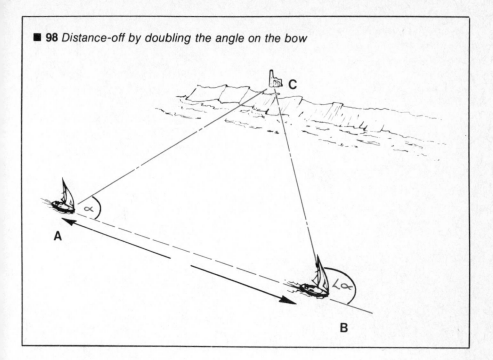

■ 98 *Distance-off by doubling the angle on the bow*

■ 99 *Distance-off by timed echo return*

METHOD 4   Distance by timed echo return ■ 99

In foggy weather a reliable estimate of the distance-off can be obtained by timing the echo of a gun or horn. The number of seconds from firing to the return of the echo times 0.09 will equal the distance in nautical miles to the point of echo return.

D = Distance-off in nautical miles

TER = timed echo return in seconds

D = TER × 0.09

Natural hand angles ■ 100, 101

When the arm is outstretched, the hand in a fist and the thumb extended, sighting across the knuckles produces an angle of approximately 10 degrees. Sighting over the tip of the thumb gives an angle of about 15 degrees.

When the hand is held flat, fingers and thumb spread wide, the basic angles of a right triangle can be roughly estimated. To sight with these angles the hand must be held close to the face with the eye at the base of the triangle.

■ **100** *Natural hand angles*

■ **101** *Natural hand angles*

Distillation

See also: Solar still, Water

Materials

A stove.

A large pot.

A metal funnel (plastic will probably melt).

A length of pipe or tubing. In emergencies, this can be taken from the engine or the boat's water system.

Some cloth, rags or a towel.

Procedure ■ **102**

Cover the pot with the funnel and attach the tubing to the small end.

Wrap the cloth or rags around the tubing.

Fill the pot with salt water and place it on the stove. As the water boils, pour cool seawater over the rags or cloth.

■ **102** *Fresh water by distillation*

Principle

When the water boils, the steam rises into the funnel and the tubing where it is condensed by contact with the cool metal. The 'fresh' water drips out the end of the tube.

NOTE:

If the water still tastes salty, repeat the distillation process a second time.

Distress signals

See also: Danger, Disabled, Help!, Medical assistance

EPIRB

The most effective distress signal is an emergency position-indicating radio beacon (EPIRB). It should be aboard before any emergency arises. It is small, self-contained and inexpensive.

A gun

A shot or other explosive signal fired at intervals of about a minute.

A fog-signaling apparatus

A continuous sounding.

Rockets or shells throwing red stars

Fired one at a time at short intervals.

SOS $\cdots - - - \cdots$

Sent out by radiotelegraph or any other signaling means.

MAYDAY

Sent out by radiotelephone or any other means.

Broadcasting the spoken word. MAYDAY, MAYDAY, MAYDAY, – Boat's name 3 times – MAYDAY, MAYDAY, MAYDAY, – Ship's position – MAYDAY, MAYDAY, MAYDAY

FLAGS

International code signal of distress:

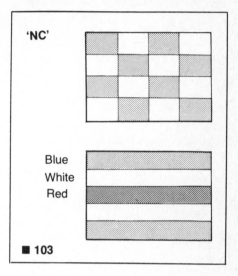

'NC'

Blue
White
Red

■ 103

or

Flying the national ensign upside down.

or

A square flag having above or below it a ball, or anything resembling a ball.

Flames

Burning oily rags in a bucket.

Rags or any rubber material can be tied to a boathook or oar, soaked in diesel or paraffin, lighted, and held outboard.

Red flares

Either parachute flares or hand-held.

A smoke signal giving off orange-colored smoke

A dye marker

When released it will spread a colored stain on the water.

An emergency position indicating radio beacon

A hand signal

Slowly and repeatedly raising and lowering arms outstretched to each side.

Other distress signals on small craft

The ensign hoisted upside down.

The ensign made fast high in the rigging.

Rags or clothing tied to a raised oar.

Acknowledgment of a distress signal

By day

An orange smoke signal.

Three white stars – possibly accompanied by bangs (thunderflashes) – fired at one-minute intervals.

By night

Three single white star rockets at one-minute intervals.

By aircraft

By day

Rocking its wings from side to side.

By night

A series of green flashes with a signal lamp.

If the message is received but not understood

By day

The aircraft will make a complete circle in a clockwise direction.

By night

A series of red flashes with a signal lamp.

Diving signals

International Code of Signals

'A'

ALPHA

'DIVERS DOWN.'

'KEEP WELL CLEAR AND AT A SLOW SPEED.'

White   Blue

For the diver   'I AM O.K.'   'I NEED ASSISTANCE.'

■ 104

Docking

See: Berthing

Doctor

See: Medical emergencies

Drogue

See: Sea anchors

Drowning

See: Artificial respiration

Drying out

See also: Aground

Alongside

While the boat is fully afloat, slacken the mooring lines and heel the boat against the quay. A 10-degree list should be enough ■ 107.

Methods to heel the boat ■ 106

Pass a strop around the mast, supported by the halyard. Clap a snatchblock to the strop. Make fast one of a line to a strong point on the dock, then drop the bight of the line to the snatchblock. Haul the snatchblock to the spreaders with the halyard and take a strain on the line to heel the vessel, taking care that the spreaders are not damaged.

Attach one end of a warp to a snatchblock or bight riding on a lower shroud or taut halyard. Attach the other end to a strong point ashore. In this manner a constant tension is maintained as the boat rises and falls.

Lay the movable ballast along the dockside deck.

■ 106 *Drying out alongside*

■ 107 *Drying out alongside*

Weights, such as anchors, can be shackled to the mooring lines to keep a constant dockside pull.

An inflatable can be placed on the deck and filled with water.

See: Careening

WARNING:

Before the boat dries out, if possible check the bottom for rocks or other obstacles.

Be ready to unshackle the upper shroud and attach chafing gear in case it touches the dock ■ **107**.

On board boats with short keels keep movement to a minimum, as they can easily tip forward.

Drying out heeled over ■ 108

Heel the boat toward the high side of the bank, most likely the shoreward side. This will probably mean heeling in the *opposite* direction from when trying to break free.
See: Aground for different methods of heeling the boat.

Move or secure any items such as batteries, lockers, or galley equipment which might be damaged when the boat is laid over.

Seal the fuel and water tanks.

Pump the bilges while the boat is still upright.

Close the portholes, cockpit lockers and sink drains.

■ **108** *Protecting the hull as she dries out*

As the water recedes, check the bottom for obstacles.

Protect the vulnerable parts of the hull with fenders, mattresses, sails or an inflatable. Lay floorboards or spars against any obstacles such as rocks or stones.

At low water, lay out a strong anchor in the direction of deep water so that when the tide rises the boat can be hauled free.

WARNING:

Do not heel bilge keel hulls, but for stability pivot them so the bow or stern points up the bank.

NOTE:

If the boat is lying on her beam ends, she must be made watertight. Tape all portholes and cockpit lockers closed. If the boat is lying toward the wind or in a downhill position, lash a sail or awning over the cockpit.

■ **109** *Drying out on beam ends*

Makeshift legs ■ 110

These can be made from booms, spinnaker or jib poles or even driftwood.

Each leg must be well lashed to the chain plates, or failing those, the turnbuckles of the lower shrouds and the deck stanchions. Disconnect lower shrouds from chain plates and rig tackles from chain plates to top of legs.

Each leg must be guyed fore and aft.

The two legs need to be lashed together with a cross bar which is also lashed to the mast.

If the bottom is muddy lay flat 'feet' under the keel and legs. These can be made from metal jerry cans, floorboards, or locker doors. They can be slid under the legs as the boat dries out, or better still, they should be lashed to the legs.

NOTE:

Anchors should be laid out, fore and aft, to prevent the boat from ranging as the tide comes in.

■ 110 *Makeshift legs*

An alarm system for grounding at night ■ 111, 112

Drop a weight attached to a line over the side until it hangs 4–8in. (10–20cm.) below the keel.

Run the line through a block to the cockpit or skylight where the end secures a pot or pan in place ■ **112.**

When the weight touches ground, the line slackens and the pan crashes to the deck.

An alarm for grounding at night

■ **111**

■ **112**

Ears

Water in the ear

Treatment

In most cases the water will drain by gravity when the person is lying on his side.

If not, gently work a piece of cotton wool into the ear with a twisting motion.

NOTE:

Do not put any sharp objects in the ear.

Pain

More than likely this is caused by an infection in the ear itself.

Treatment

A few drops of warmed, but not hot, olive oil can have a soothing effect.

Take antibiotics. **See: Antibiotics**

Foreign body in the ear

Pull the ear *up* and *back* which makes it possible to see far into the ear. If the object can be seen, remove it carefully with a pair of tweezers.

Insects in the ear

Put a drop or two of olive or cooking oil, alcohol, or spirits – rum or whisky – in the ear which should kill the insect. Then, remove carefully with tweezers.

Echo sounder

METHOD 1   Depth equals position
■ 113

If lost

While holding a steady course, make a series of soundings – at least a half dozen – at regular intervals, for example, every quarter or half hour, and record the distance traveled. Do not forget to correct soundings for Tide. **See: NOTE** page 75

Plot the soundings on a sheet of tracing paper using the same scale as the chart. Then attempt to align the tracing over the chart until the line of soundings matches the soundings on the chart.

If sailing on a known course

Make a series of soundings – at least half a dozen – at regular intervals, and record the distance traveled. Do not forget to correct all soundings for Tide. **See: NOTE** page 75

Plot the soundings on a sheet of tracing paper using the same scale as the chart. Place the tracing over the chart and align it along your course. When the soundings are matched with those of the charted depths, the last sounding along the line becomes a 'fix' ■ 114.

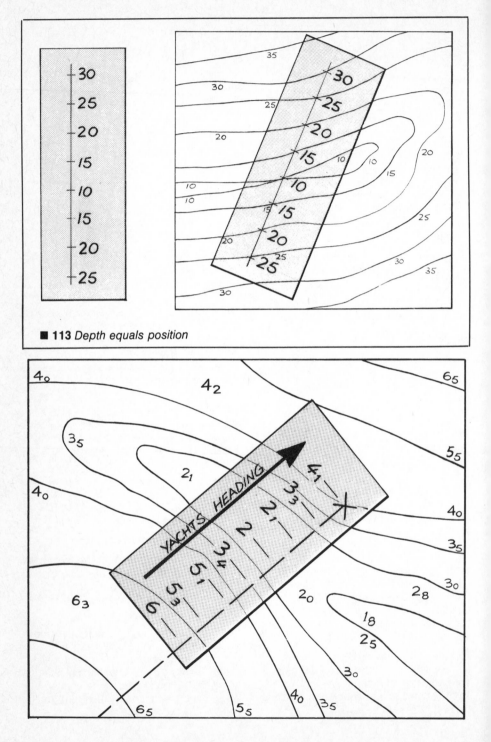

■ **113** *Depth equals position*

METHOD 2 'Running down' a fathom line (contour navigation) ■ 115

Once a charted fathom line (contour line) – corrected for Tide **(See: NOTE** below) – is crossed, its direction can be determined by making a series of short tacks. One can then 'run down' or follow the line in much the same manner as old captains once 'ran down' latitude lines to their destinations. In this case, however, the course tacks across the fathom line, thus maintaining contact and following it to a known point.

NOTE:

Before using an echo sounder reading for navigational calculations allowance must be made for:

1 – The distance from the transducer to the surface of the water.

2 – Tide.

In tidal waters, charted depths are for Mean Low Water, that is, the average depth at low water which is *unlikely* to be the depth at the moment.
If the tidal range is known, this can be taken as an error factor.

or

If the tidal range and the time of tidal change is known, the approximate depth above chart datum can be calculated using the 'Law of Twelths'.

The first hour tide rises or falls by one-twelfth of its range; the second, two-twelfths; the third, three-twelfths; the fourth, three-twelfths; the fifth, two-twelfths; the sixth, one-twelfth.

METHOD 3　Character of the bottom indicates position

Occasionally, knowing the character of the seabed can help establish one's position, or conversely, where one isn't!

Soft mud ■ 116

The leading edge of the display is not clearly defined. Once spurious echoes are eliminated, the gain control will probably be set higher than for other bottoms, as soft mud is more absorbent of an ultrasonic pulse and usually returns a fairly weak echo.

Zero flash

■ 116 Echo sounder display in soft mud

Sand or gravel ■ 117

The leading edge is strong and clearly defined, and does not alter with changes in the gain control. A second, or sometimes even a third rebound echo may be visible.

Zero flash

■ 117 Echo sounder display in sand or gravel

Rocks ■ 118

The echo is elongated and broken into segments even with a low setting of the gain control. This is due to the multiple echoes which are returned from the uneven bottom surface. As the boat moves through the water, the leading edge should oscillate rapidly.

Zero flash

■ 118 Echo sounder display with a rocky bottom

Engine failure

Diesel

WARNING:

An overheated engine can quickly suffer damage. Turn it off immediately, and check:

The water inlet for blockage.

The cooling water level in the engine.

The oil level.

The fan belt to the water pump.

That the propeller is clear.

WARNING:

Any loss of oil pressure indicates a serious problem. Stop the engine. Check the oil level and refill if necessary. If there is still no pressure, let the motor cool. Then, if absolutely essential, such as coming alongside in port, run the engine for only very short periods of time.

■ **120** *The electrical system of a gasoline engine*

Touch the starter button. If there is no spark at the points as they open, there is trouble in the low-voltage circuit of the coil. Check the ignition switch.

If there is still no spark, either the coil or the condenser is defective.

Disconnect condenser from breaker points and reassemble distributor. Touch starter button. If engine fires, shut off immediately and install new condenser.

NOTE:

If the engine has not been run for a long time, and will not start, it is better to check the fuel system before the electrical system.

Checking the fuel system

1 – Unscrew the fuel line to the carburetor, and turn over the engine ■ **121A.**

If fuel comes out:

The carburetor is defective. Dismantle and clean it.

If no fuel comes out:

The fuel tank is empty.

The fuel pump is broken.

There is a leak or blockage in the line.

2 – Disconnect the intake to the fuel pump ■ **121B.**

If the fuel pump is lower than the tank and no fuel appears:

The tank is empty.

There is a leak or blockage in the line.

Suck on the line if the fuel pump is higher than the tank, and if no fuel appears:

The tank is empty.

There is a leak or blockage in the line.

If the fuel appears at the fuel pump intake:

The fuel pump is probably either broken or blocked. Dismantle and clean it.

■ **121** *The fuel system of a gasoline engine*

NOTE:

Water in the fuel tank

Small quantities of water can be burned off by mixing 1 pint ($\frac{1}{2}$ liter) of alcohol to every 210 quarts (200 liters) of fuel. The water will combine with the alcohol and be burned off in combustion.

A sediment bowl of generous proportions will trap small amounts of water. Clean it frequently.

Evacuation

See also: Abandon ship!, Distress signals

Yacht to helicopter

Procedure

Make the transfer from a dinghy or liferaft towed astern

or

Keep the boat on a predictable course.

Make the transfer from the stern.

If possible, release the backstay, and support the mast with halyards or the topping lift. **See: Rigging failure**

Wave a 'come on' hand signal when you are ready for the transfer. Use a flashlight at night.

If a litter or basket is lowered do not touch it until it makes contact with the deck as it may be charged with static electricity.

WARNING:

Do not make fast the line or wire lowered from the helicopter.

If a sick person is being transferred alone, a note explaining his condition, treatment, and any medication he has been given should accompany him. His hands and arms should be well secured to the litter.

NOTE:

If a harness is not lowered, use a bosun's chair. For emergency bosun's chairs **See: Climbing the mast**

Yacht to ship

Procedure

Approach the ship on its leeward side.

If the ship has pumped out oil

Attempt to stay in the slick.

Put out all fenders. For makeshift fenders **See: Fenders**

If a stretcher is passed from the ship

Stand off.

Secure the sick person to the stretcher, then come alongside again for the transfer.

If no stretcher is available

One may be constructed from a pipe cot, sail bags lashed to dinghy oars, or a mattress supported by oars or boathooks.

WARNING:

Be prepared to lose your mast. Take down all sail, and, if possible, remove the boom and secure it on deck.

Explosion

See: Fire

Exposure (Hypothermia)

See also: Frostbite, Drowning

Treatment

If legs or feet appear to be insensitive or 'asleep'

See: **Immersion foot**

If frozen white spots appear on the body

See: **Frostbite**

Put the survivor in a *tub* of lukewarm water, preferably about 98°F. (37°C.)

Slowly add warm water – about 108°F. (42°C.)

Keep the legs out of the water so that the body will warm up first.

If no tub is available

Lay the survivor on his back, fully clothed, and slowly and carefully pour warm water over him.

If no warm water is available

Remove the survivor's clothes, and cover him with a blanket, preheated if possible.

Serve him hot drinks with plenty of sugar.

If necessary, warm the survivor with your own body, and massage him gently.

NOTE:

Do *not* give alcohol to anyone suffering from exposure.

Eyes

Foreign body in the eye

Do *not* rub the eye!

Wash hands thoroughly before touching the eye.

Treatment

Examine the lower lid first.

If the object is there, bring the upper lid down over the lower lid, which may dislodge the object.

If this does not work, wash the eye with fresh water in an eye cup or a clean drinking glass. Hold the cup firmly against the face, tilt the head back, and roll the eye several times.

If the object is lodged on the upper lid, the lid should be inverted over a pencil or matchstick. Remove the object with a shred of clean, moistened cotton wool on the end of a toothpick.

If the object is lodged on the cornea, or if it cannot be seen, close the eye, cover with a patch of cotton or gauze and anchor shut with a piece of tape. Removal by the uninitiated can be dangerous.

If there is a suggestion of infection, treat with antibiotic ointment. **See: Antibiotics**

Chemicals in the eye

Wash the eye *continuously*, using large amounts of water. Pour the water from the inner to the outer part of the eye. Do this for several minutes. Then repeat after 15 minutes. A few drops of mineral, olive, or castor oil after copious washing will soothe any inflammation.

Fatigue

Symptoms

Lack of concentration.
Forgetfulness.
Simple 'stupid' errors.
Lack of efficiency.
Strange visual experiences, distortions or hallucinations.

Treatment

Plenty of warm clothing.

For immediate strength – sugar in the form of honey or sweets.

To prevent errors and ensure rational decisions, one should monitor one's behavior by introspection, speaking out loud, or listing on paper carefully what is to be done next.

Medication

'Stay-awake' pills*

	Dosage
England Dexamphetamine Sulfate	1 tablet 5mg. 2 times/day
Germany Captagon	½–1 tablet 1–2 times/day
U.S. NoDoz	1–2 tablets 2–3 times/day

Amphetamines are almost unobtainable in France and the U.S.

Fenders

In emergencies use ■ 122

Rubber tires ■ **122A.**

Lifejackets.

Pillows in sailbags ■ **122B.**

Sealed detergent bottles or plastic water containers ■ **122C.**

Cockpit cushions ■ **122D.**

Mattresses.

NOTE:

For squeaky fenders, pour a little dish-washing liquid over them. This will also form a protective film against oil and pollution in the water.

Home-made fenders ■ 123

Materials

7ft. (2m.) of heavy rope.

A piece of foam rubber such as that cut from a cushion or pillow.

8sq.ft. (1sq.m.) of canvas.

Needle and thread.

Procedure

Knot the two ends of the rope and triple the loop ■ **123A.**

Wrap the foam around it and bind it in place ■ **123B, 123C.**

Cover with canvas. Sew the seams and the ends to the rope ■ **123D.**

■ **122** *Makeshift fenders*

■ **123** *A home-made fender*

Ferrocement repair

Cracks

All breaks in the hull, even scratches, should be repaired immediately to prevent water from entering and rusting the mesh.

A patching putty can be made from epoxy, sand and water.

If rust stains have already appeared, the damaged area should be scraped back to the mesh before patching.

For superficial rust a wire brushing is sufficient.

Clean away loose concrete with a paint scraper or screwdriver.

Sand any exposed mesh.

Fill with the epoxy-sand putty.

Fiberglass repair

Cracks ■ 124, 125

If necessary, widen the crack so that it will hold a repair putty ■ 124.

Extend each end of the break about ³/₈in. (1cm.) to relieve any stress.

Clean away all dust.

Mix gelcoat, resin, hardener and loose bits of fiberglass mat into a paste or putty.

Fill the crack and press the putty in with a knife.

Leave some excess on top as the putty tends to shrink slightly when drying.

Cover the area with a plastic sheet and tape it down tightly since gelcoat will not cure properly if exposed to the air ■ 125.

NOTE:

When working with fiberglass one should *always* wear gloves.

Holes

METHOD 1   Temporary patching
■ 126

Make a patch from thin marine plywood, copper or tin sheeting, or metal from an unrolled tin, such as an oil or fruit can. Cut the patch so that it overlaps the hole by at least three fingers' width.

Drill holes in the patch first, then use it as a template to make holes in the hull. The holes should not be more than four fingers apart.

Use a thick coating of mastic for a gasket or, failing that, an old towel, sail cloth, or rags well greased with heavy lubricating grease or soaked in paint.

Bolt the patch in place, using plywood or pieces of metal as washers on the inside.

If the hole is bigger than fist size

An inside and outside patch will be necessary. In this case, the patches should be reinforced with a plank, then bolted to each other *through* the hole, which will also help to hold them rigid.

■ 124

Repairing cracks in fiberglass

■ 125

■ **126** *A temporary patch for a fiberglass hull*

METHOD 2   A fiberglass patch

If possible, make the patch from the inside of the hull.

With a saw, cut away all of the damaged area, until only unfractured material is showing.

Round the hole, if possible ■ **127.**

■ **127** *A fiberglass patch*

Bevel the edges inwards with a file ■ **128B.**

On the outside, sand the area 2–4in. (5–10cm.) around the hole.

On the inside, sand the area 4–6in. (10–15cm.) around the hole.

Dust the area well.

Make a backing plate from metal sheeting, linoleum, or, if necessary, cardboard covered with cellophane. This plate should be at least 4in. (10cm.) larger than the hole, and should be securely taped on the outside of the hull.

Cut the fiberglass cloth or mat to cover the hole and overlap at least 2in. (5cm.). Different layers should be crisscrossed.

Saturate the fiberglass patch with resin-hardener mix and then lay it in place.

Remove all air bubbles as these could become weak points in the patch ■ **128C.**

NOTE:

Hardening time is dependent upon air temperature, the exact mix of hardener and resin and the thickness of the patch.

Increase hardening time by raising temperature.

■ **128**

Fire

See also: Abandon ship!, Evacuation, Distress signals

International Code of Signals

'J'

JULIET

'I AM ON FIRE AND HAVE
DANGEROUS CARGO ON BOARD,
KEEP WELL CLEAR OF ME!'

Blue
White
Blue

■ 129

In light winds

Drop all sails and stop the boat.

In strong winds

Sail downwind immediately. (The object being to minimize the apparent wind as quickly as possible.)

Fire-fighting

Wet your clothes.

Direct the fire extinguisher toward the base of the fire, not toward the flames.

Cushions and mattresses afire

They should be thrown overboard.

Fiberglass

Water should be used in conjunction with fire extinguishers to cool the material, as hot fiberglass can easily catch fire again.

Gasoline and oil

Sprayed water will *not* extinguish the fire, but will help to cool the area and prevent the flames from spreading. Water may float burning gasoline to other parts of the vessel.

Engines

Throw a wet blanket or towel over it and attempt to suffocate the flames.

A person on fire ■ 130

Throw him over the side, *or*

Lay him on the deck.

Stand at his head holding a wet blanket or towel in front of you. Secure the corners with your feet, then fall forward over the burning man.

If a person's clothing is on fire and a fire extinguisher is your only resort, do not point it at any exposed part of the body, particularly the eyes, since CO_2 can cause freezer burn.

■ **130** *A person on fire.*

When opening a door

Crouch low, as the flames and heat will tend to rise. Also visibility is better near the deck ■ **131.**

■ 131

When opening a hatch

Do so from the side with the hinges ■ **132.**

NOTE:

Those not involved in fire-fighting, should ready the dinghy and liferaft and leave the boat.

■ 132

To take survivors from a burning boat

METHOD 1

Approach the boat from windward, bow to bow, if possible. This will lessen the impact should the fuel tanks explode. In general, the force of a boat tank explosion is directed upwards by the shape of the hull.

METHOD 2

Tow or drift a dinghy or inflated liferaft close to the other boat on a long line. Let the survivors climb on board, then haul them to you.

For treatment of burns **See: Burns**

The fire-fighting principle

Three elements are necessary to support any fire:

Oxygen – Fuel – High temperature.

These can be thought of as constructing a fire triangle.

Eliminate any side, and the fire will go out.

Oxygen   Fuel

Fire

High temperature

Fish

See also: Fishing, Poisoned fish

Poisonous fish ■ 133, 134, 135, 136

In general, these species have proportionally large teeth or beaks as they often feed on coral. Hence, scavengers who feed on them may also be poisonous.

WARNING:

Do not eat any fish which puff up like balloons when caught.

■ **133** *Triggerfish*

■ **134** *Filefish*

■ **135** *Puffer (uninflated)*

■ **136** *Puffer (inflated)*

Venomous fish ■ 137, 138, 139, 140, 141, 142

These fish can usually be identified by their spiny appearance. This often includes bristles and veil-like appendages.

If in doubt, do not touch or eat them.

■ **138** *Scorpion fish*

■ **142** *Stingray*

■ **137** *Zebra or turkey fish*

■ **140** *Stonefish*

■ **139** *Toadfish*

■ **141** *Porcupine fish*

Fishhook injuries

Removing a fishhook from another person

METHOD 1 ■ 143

Place the hand on a hard surface, palm up.

Loop the line around the curve of the hook, and wind the ends several times around your forefinger.

With the other hand, grip the eye of the hook, and push it down to disengage the barb.

Align the string with the shank's long axis, and *yank hard*.

NOTE:

If necessary, the entire operation can be done one-handed.

■ 143

METHOD 2 ■ 144

Insert a hypodermic needle along the barbed side of the hook, with the beveled part of the point towards the inside of the hook's curve.

Pull gently on the shank to disengage the barb.

Then, push the needle gently downwards until its hole locks over the barb.

Rotate the hook shank slightly downwards and the hook curve upwards until the needle and hook are removed through the original wound.

METHOD 3 ■ 145

Cut off the eye of the hook with a pair of wire cutters.

Push the shaft *into* the flesh until the pointed, barbed end comes out of the skin.

Grip it firmly, then pull the shaft through the wound and out.

■ 144

Clean the wound thoroughly and cover with antiseptic. **See: Antiseptic**

If signs of infection appear – pain, redness and swelling **See: Antibiotics**

■ 145

Fishing

See also: Fish, Fishhook injuries, Poisoned fish

Emergency fishing gear ■ 146, 147, 148, 149

Lures

These can be manufactured from unraveled pieces of rope, strips of plastic bag, silver paper, bright-colored rags, feathers or the skin or entrails of a fish. If possible, a wire leader should be attached to the hook, and the lure constructed around it ■ 146, 147, 148.

A spinner can be fashioned from a tin or beer can. In this case, the hook must be screwed, bolted or wired to the pieces of metal ■ 149.

In general, yellow, white or silver lures are best early in the morning or at sunset, brightly colored ones during the day.

Makeshift lure

■ 146   ■ 147   ■ 148   ■ 149

Makeshift hook

■ 150   ■ 151   ■ 152   ■ 153

Hooks ■ 150, 151, 152, 153

These can be manufactured from such items as pins, knives, shoe nails, fish bones, pencil clips, tins or a bent fork.

Fishing knots ■ 154, 155

A single blood knot.

Tying the line to a swivel.

After tying the half hitches pull the knot tight. It will draw up into a neat roll.

NOTE: ■ 156

Many survivors of liferaft ordeals report the most effective means of catching fish is to gaff or harpoon those beneath the raft. A harpoon can be fabricated by lashing a knife to the end of a paddle, and a gaff by lashing on a large fishhook.

■ 154   ■ 155

■ 156 *A makeshift harpoon and gaff*

Fishing line

Small lengths of moderately strong line can be improvised from shoe laces, strips of cloth, a belt, or woven from unraveled rope or fabric.

Fish trap ■ 157

This can be fabricated from a sea anchor, paddles and light clothing, or a bucket with holes in it.

NOTE:

Many types of fish are attracted to light, even of low intensity. On a moonlit night even a mirror reflecting the moonlight on the water can be effective.

Drying marine food

The flesh of most marine animals can be dried in the sun and, if kept dry, preserved for months.

When cut into strips of not more than $\frac{3}{4}$in. (2cm.) thickness, the meat should dry within four days. It can be eaten at any stage in the drying process.

For quicker drying, the meat can be shredded into small pieces, and then either laid on trays or hung on lengths of twine.

Drying fish

For small fish (less than 6lb. or 2kg.)
■ 158

Chop off the heads and tails.

Clean.

Break the backbones so that the fish are flat.

Lay them in the sun, and sprinkle on some salt.

Then string the fish on a line between the shrouds until they become hard.

Store below, either in an open-weave basket or hanging between deck beams.

To use:

Soak the pieces in fresh water for a day, changing the water at least twice.

For larger fish

De-bone as much as possible.

Cut into strips or fillets.

Then, follow the same procedure as for smaller fish.

Drying shark meat

Cut the meat into fillets.

Soak in a strong brine solution for at least

■ **157** *Makeshift fish traps*

a day, changing the water several times.

When the 'shark' smell is gone, hang up to dry in the same manner as any other fish.

Drying crab and lobster

Boil in seawater for 10 minutes.

Remove from the shell.

Shred the meat with your fingers, then lay it out in thin layers on trays or plates.

Place them in the sun, and turn the meat every hour or two. In two days the meat should be well dried and ready for storage.

Drying shrimp

Boil in seawater for 10 minutes.

Take off the shells and heads, and cut away the veins.

Arrange the meat on plates or trays.

Place them in the sun, and turn the meat every hour or two. In 3–4 days the meat should be well dried and ready for storage.

■ 158 *Drying fish between the shrouds*

Flares

See also: Distress signals

ORANGE SMOKE – Distress

RED – Distress

WHITE – Warning of imminent danger, such as collision

or

Acknowledgment of a distress signal

GREEN – Special signals, often used by the Navy and by searching aircraft

BLUE – Request for a pilot

Firing

Flares should be held at arm's length, pointing away so that the dross does not drip onto hands or body.

For maximum effect, flares should be fired *downwind*.

Flares should be fired in groups of two, the second a minute or two after the first.

Range at night

A hand-held flare – about five miles.

A parachute flare – about 20–25 miles.

A star shell – about 10 miles.

Emergency flares

Oil-soaked rags burning in a bucket.

Burning plastic material, such as polystyrene and mattress and cushion stuffings.

WARNING:

As a general rule, flares have a three-year life span, if stored in dry conditions. The magnesium powder used in firing slowly deteriorates and beyond three years cannot be considered reliable.

Flooding

See: Holes

Fog

Warning signs

The air becomes extremely moist and clammy.

Brightwork, cabin windows and portholes steam with condensation.

Smoke tends to lie in the sky in long layered lines.

Lights take on a distinct halo effect.

Changes appear in the color of the cloud base.

Principle

Sea fog is nothing more than a cloud resting on the surface of the water, which is formed by the meeting of cold air and warm water or the reverse. The most common type is *advection fog*, that is, the passage of a current of warm air over the colder surface of the sea. As the air is cooled, a temperature inversion takes place, and when the air is cooled below the dew point, condensation occurs and water vapor appears in the form of fog.

This kind of fog is quite common near coasts where a warm off-shore air current encounters a cooler sea. Should that air current be humid, often it creates a dense layer of fog on the sea, while 13 or 15ft. (4 or 5 meters) above it the warmer air is completely clear. In this kind of fog one encounters ships with the tops of their masts pointed into a clear sky and their decks a foggy gloom.

If in congested waters or shipping lanes

Lifejackets should be worn.

The liferaft straps should be unlashed.

A radar reflector hoisted no less than 13ft. (4 meters) above the deck. **See: Radar reflectors**

If conditions permit, the dinghy can be towed astern.

Visibility scale used in weather forecasts

	Visibility
Fog	Less than 3,300ft. (1,000 meters)
Mist (Humidity more than 95%)	3,300–6,600ft. (1,000 to 2,000 meters)
Haze (Humidity less than 95%)	3,300–6,600ft. (1,000 to 2,000 meters)
Poor	6,600ft. (2,000 meters) to 2 nautical miles
Moderate	2–5.5 miles
Good	over 5 miles

Distances in fog

In dense fog, distances can be difficult to judge. Crumpling a sheet of newspaper into a ball, throwing it over the side, and watching it float out of sight will give some idea as to the limits of visibility. However, fog is seldom uniform in density. A horizon of 950ft. (300 meters) can double or triple, or halve, from one moment to the next.

A lookout should try vantage points as high and low as possible as in patches he may be able to see under or over the bank. If the fog is shallow, the first sighting of another vessel could be high in the air – a bridge or crosstrees appearing to float on a whispy cloud.
See also: Distance at sea

Sound in fog

In foggy conditions, sounds are often deflected, diminished or amplified, even to such an extent that the ring of a buoy's bell can appear to grow weaker the closer one approaches it, or the grunt of a diaphone seems to be nearer than a whistle when it is actually twice as far away. Also, it is quite possible to have one impression of direction and intensity on deck and another aloft.

There are no hard and fast rules.

A lookout should always keep in mind the possibility, especially if the fog is light and patchy, that the lighthouse, lightship or buoy that he is straining to hear may be experiencing a completely clear day and thus not sending out a signal.

If you *must* depend on acoustic bearings, the following method has proved reliable. Stand, eyes closed, holding a hand-bearing compass, and turn slowly until convinced you are facing sound source. Open your eyes and read the bearing. Repeat two more times. If the readings are consistent, they may be relied on.

NOTE:

If worse comes to worst, take an acoustic bearing by standing on deck with your eyes closed and with a hand-bearing compass in hand. Adjust position until certain you are facing object. Take bearing on compass. Repeat several times for several objects.

Types and characteristics of fog signals

Type (Chart abbreviation given in brackets)
        Characteristic

Type	Characteristic
Diaphone (Dia)	Strong note of low tone ending with easily distinguished grunt
Siren (Siren)	Medium-powered high or low note or both together
Reed (Reed)	Lower powered than siren with high note. May be hand operated using little power
Tyfon (Tyfon)	Powerful medium-pitched note similar to a ship's fog signal
Nautophone (Nauto)	High note similar to Reed
Diaphragm horn	Powerful medium-pitched note. Several sound frequencies produced simultaneously
Gun (Gun)	Explosive signals from a gun. An acetylene gun gives a brilliant flash at the time of the explosion (not used in U.S.)
Explosive (Explos)	Signals explode in mid-air. Usually placed in outlying positions (not used in U.S.)
Bell (Bell)	wa=wave actuated. Notes may be of any pitch depending on size of bell
Whistle (Whis)	Usually placed on isolated buoys
Gong (Gong)	Occasionally used at pier ends, etc.

Sound signals in restricted visibility

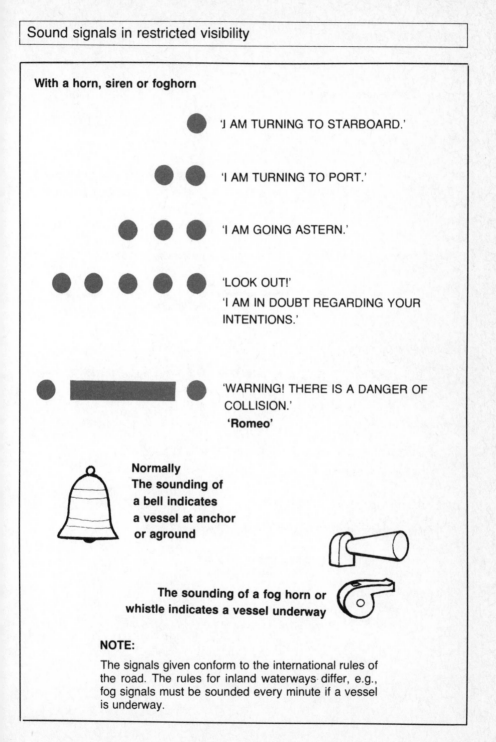

With a horn, siren or foghorn

●   'I AM TURNING TO STARBOARD.'

● ●   'I AM TURNING TO PORT.'

● ● ●   'I AM GOING ASTERN.'

● ● ● ● ●   'LOOK OUT!'
'I AM IN DOUBT REGARDING YOUR INTENTIONS.'

● ▬▬▬▬ ●   'WARNING! THERE IS A DANGER OF COLLISION.'
'Romeo'

**Normally
The sounding of
a bell indicates
a vessel at anchor
or aground**

**The sounding of a fog horn or
whistle indicates a vessel underway**

NOTE:

The signals given conform to the international rules of
the road. The rules for inland waterways differ, e.g.,
fog signals must be sounded every minute if a vessel
is underway.

Vessels underway

Power vessel underway

▬▬ 2 minutes ▬▬ 2 minutes ▬▬

Power vessel underway – but stopped and making no way through the water

▬▬ ▬▬2 minutes▬▬ ▬▬ 2 minutes▬▬ ▬▬

Vessel fishing, towing, restricted in ability to maneuver, or a sailing boat on any tack

▬▬ ● ● 2 minutes ▬▬ ● ● 2 minutes ▬▬ ● ●

Last vessel in a tow

▬▬ ● ● ●2 minutes▬▬ ● ● ●2 minutes▬▬ ● ● ●

Pilot vessel making way

▬▬ ● ● ● ●2 minutes ▬▬ ● ● ● ●2 minutes
● ● ● ● ▬▬

Pilot vessel stopped but not at anchor

▬▬ ▬▬ ● ● ●2 minutes ▬▬ ▬▬ ● ● ●2 minutes
▬▬ ▬▬ ● ● ●

Pilot vessel on duty

● ● ● ●

NOTE:

Fishing boats have no special anchor
signals in fog.

A vessel aground

The bell – and gong – signals are
preceded and followed by three strokes of
the bell.

3 strokes   5 seconds   3 strokes

1 minute   1 minute

NOTE:

If the vessel aground is longer than 365ft.
(100 meters) a gong is sounded rapidly
for five seconds after the ringing of the
bell.

Vessels at anchor

Ship at anchor

5 seconds   5 seconds   5 seconds

1 minute   1 minute

Ship at anchor more than 365ft. (100 meters) in length

5 seconds 5 seconds   5 seconds 5 seconds   5 seconds 5 seconds

1 minute   1 minute

Pilot ship at anchor

5 seconds 4 short blasts   5 seconds 4 short blasts   5 seconds 4 short blasts

1 minute   1 minute

Oil rig at anchor

● ● ▬▬▬   30 seconds ● ● ▬▬▬   30 seconds ● ● ▬▬▬

'U'   'U'   'U'

Forestay

See: Rigging failures

Fractures

See also: Shock

Fracture of the extremities

Symptoms

Swelling of the limb.

The limb is out of alignment.

Intense pain.

Treatment

See: Shock

Immobilize the limb with a splint – sail batten, boathook, etc.

If the fracture is within the joint, immobilize the entire limb until proper medical help can be found.

Medication

See: Pain killers, Tranquilizers

Skull fracture

Symptoms

A depressed area on the skull (which may be hidden by a bruise).

Blood or fluid draining from the nose, ears or mouth.

Difficulty swallowing.

The pupils of the eyes may be unequal in size.

Loss of consciousness.

Drowsiness.

Vomiting.

A change in behavior.

NOTE:

Symptoms such as loss of consciousness, drowsiness and vomiting may appear up to 24 hours after the injury.

Treatment

Let the fluids continue to drain by putting the head forward. Take ampicillin. **See: Antibiotics**

Clean the wound and stitch it if necessary. **See: Wounds**

Wrap the wound with a *loose*, fluffy dressing.

Keep the victim warm, quiet and immobilized until medical help can be found.

Medication

See: Pain killers but do *not* use narcotics for a head injury.

See: Tranquilizers – administer only if absolutely necessary as they may mask the symptoms.

Fractures of the spine

Symptoms

Any injury to the back should be regarded as a possible fracture of the spine.

Paralysis.

A deformed spine.

NOTE:

If the person is unconscious, prick the toes or fingers. No reflex indicates paralysis.

Treatment

Immobilization – The person should be moved *only if absolutely necessary*, and then retaining *complete body alignment*. Even if the injury appears to be slight, movement should be restricted, as it may cause paralysis.

Frostbite

See also: Exposure

Symptoms

The frozen part will be white and numb.

NOTE:
Frostbite occurs most often on the nose, cheeks ears, toes and fingers.

Treatment

The frozen part should be thawed as quickly as possible by:

Immersing it in water which is at normal body temperature (about 98°F., or 37°C.)

or

Wrapping it in warm blankets.

NOTE:

Massage should be avoided as it may damage tissue. Also, the frozen part *should not* be rubbed with snow or cold water as has been formerly advocated as an emergency treatment.

When the part thaws, it should be exercised.

Do not remove any dead tissue unless it is badly infected.

Blisters that form should not be disturbed.

No weight should be put on the injured part.

Take pain killers as necessary. **See: Pain killers**

For infection, take antibiotics. **See: Antibiotics**

G

Gale

See: Heavy weather

Grounding

See: Aground

Gasoline engine

See: Engine failure — gasoline

GRP repair

See: Fiberglass repair

H

Hemorrhages

See also: Shock, wounds

To stop bleeding

Apply continuous pressure to the site.

Do this for at least 10 minutes in order to give the clot time to form, or longer if necessary.

If the bleeding is severe

Attempt to control it by pressing on a pressure point ■ **159**.

Apply a tourniquet as a last resort.

If the bleeding is pulsing

An artery has been severed.

If the bleeding cannot be controlled by direct pressure

Apply a tourniquet between the wound and the heart. Release it gradually for a few seconds as the bleeding stops.

If it doesn't stop bleeding

The artery must be tied off. **See: Wounds**

Should it be necessary to leave the tourniquet on, it must be released for a few seconds every 15 minutes – in cold weather, every 10 minutes.

NOTE:

If the person loses a large amount of blood, he may go into shock and require a transfusion. **See: Shock**

■ **159** *Pressure points used to control bleeding*

Heart failure

See: Artificial respiration

Heat exhaustion

See also: Sunstroke

Symptoms

Skin is pale and moist.

NOTE:

By contrast, in a condition of *sunstroke* the skin is dry, flushed and hot.

Weakness.

Headache.

Often nausea and vomiting.

Treatment

Rest in a cool place.

The head should be lowered.

Drink plenty of fluids.

Take extra salt.

For a weak pulse – strong black coffee.

Heaving to

Purpose

To cope with a storm by 'stopping' or retarding the movement of the boat.

As a general rule one should *heave to under sail,* then, as conditions worsen – seas rise, wind gains force or the boat heels dangerously – either take down all sails and *lie ahull, lie ahull to a sea anchor*, or at that point decide to run with the storm. **See: Running**

For maximum 'stopping' power, such as may be necessary *on a lee shore: ride to a sea anchor.*

WARNING:

Boats with long, straight keels usually heave to more easily than short fin keels.

Some modern designs have great difficulty heaving to under sail and may require someone at the helm or another tactic must be chosen.

Heaving to under sail

See: Stormsails

The jib is backed, sheeted to windward.

A reefed mainsail or trysail is sheeted amidships.

The helm is lashed alee.

The force of the mainsail and the rudder is counterbalanced by the backed jib. When the bow comes up into the wind, the jib causes the boat to fall off. The rudder and mainsail drive the boat ahead, and the cycle is repeated ■ **160.**

WARNING:

Even hove-to under sail, the boat may easily make 1–2 knots headway.

NOTE:

When lashing the tiller use strong shock

■ *160 Heaving to under sail*

cords or elastic nylon line leaving the rudder a little play to prevent damage.

Heaving to under sail can usually be accomplished by any of several sail plans. Which one depends upon such factors as hull shape, windage, and rigging. The following combinations have been used successfully:

Sloops with a small fore-triangle

1 – A backed storm-jib and a reefed mainsail or trysail sheeted in ■ **162.**

2 – A backed storm staysail and a riding sail (a storm-jib hanked on the backstay and sheeted in) ■ **162.**

3 – Only a riding sail ■ **161.**

4 – Only a trysail.

Sloop with a large fore-triangle

1 – Only a backed jib ■ **163.**

2 – Only a riding sail.

3 – A backed storm staysail and a riding sail.

Traditional cutter

1 – A close-hauled storm-jib, backed staysail and a reefed mainsail ■ **164.**

2 – A backed spitfire jib and a storm trysail.

3 – A backed storm staysail and a storm trysail.

■ **161** *A sloop heaving to*

■ **162** *A sloop heaving to*

■ **163** *A sloop heaving to*

■ **164** *A cutter heaving to*

Ketch

1 – Only a reefed mizzen.

2 – A backed jib and a reefed mizzen ■ **165.**

3 – Only a storm trysail.

4 – A backed jib and a reefed mainsail.

Yawl

1 – Only a storm trysail ■ **166.**

2 – A backed jib and the mizzen well sheeted in.

3 – Only a reefed mizzen.

4 – A backed jib and a reefed mainsail.

WARNING:

When heaving to with only the riding sail or mizzen and the helm lashed down, the boat should *not* lie too close to the wind. There is a danger of being thrown backwards by a wave and damaging the rudder.

Schooner

1 – Only a reefed foresail.

2 – A storm fore-staysail and a main stormsail or a reefed down mainsail ■ **167.**

NOTE:

To find the correct rudder angle, some experimentation will be necessary.

■ **165** *A ketch heaving to*

■ **166** *A yawl heaving to*

■ **167** *A schooner heaving to*

Lying ahull or hulling

All sail is taken down.

The helm is lashed to leeward.

The boat takes up 'her own' position with respect to the seas.

Leaving the boat to fend for herself is not considered bad seamanship. Quite the contrary. It is a tactic to be employed when the wind is too strong to carry sail. Although the boat will probably lie nearly beam-on to the seas, the rolling motion will be more uncomfortable than dangerous.

The boat will move gradually at 1–2 knots to leeward and also make some headway due to the windage of the hull and rigging.

The *danger* in lying ahull is that a freak wave will catch the boat, throw her on her side, damage the superstructure, or even capsize her.

Therefore, *if the waves reach dangerous heights the decision must be made to run with the storm.* **See: Running**

Lying ahull/riding to a sea anchor ■ 168

This provides maximum 'stopping' power.

The sea anchor may be streamed from either the bow or the stern.

A jib may be sheeted amidships or hanked on the backstay as a riding sail.

A sea anchor is a brutal brake against the seas which can produce a tremendous strain on the boat and, in effect, robs it of some buoyancy.

When a sea anchor is streamed from the stern, the boat is in danger of being pooped or pitch-poled.

When a sea anchor is streamed from the bow, the boat can easily be thrown backwards and the rudder damaged.

A sea anchor should only be used when the boat no longer has sea room, for example, on a lee shore.

For sea anchor techniques **See: Sea anchor**

Heavy weather

If you think heavy weather is on the horizon, you are already in it

A heavy weather check-list

Reef or change the sails.

Clear the deck and lash down all gear – don't trust elastic bands or snap fittings.

Check the lifelines and rig jackstays: **See: Safety harness**

Put on safety harnesses.

Record the last known position and the barometer reading.

Prepare the sea anchor and warps.

Below: secure all lockers, especially those in the galley and holding tools and spares.

Empty bilge and clear cockpit drains.

Start the engine for a quick check, then close off the fuel line and the seacocks.

Close all other seacocks, ventilators and exhausts, and the hawse pipe.

Secure the stormboards.

Put on all hatch covers.

Rig leeboards for the berths.

Start a pot of stew simmering.

A decision must be made to:

1 – Continue on course under reduced sail. **See: Reefing and sail reduction, Stormsails**

2 – Head for port or shelter under reduced sail.

3 – Cope immediately by either:

■ **168** *Streaming a sea anchor*

1 – Heaving to

Attempting to 'stop' or retard the movement of the boat or

2 – Running

Allowing the boat to move with the storm, with or without a device, such as warps or a sea anchor, to slow her down.

If there is a possibility that a revolving storm – cyclone, hurricane or typhoon – is approaching See: Law of storms

NOTE:

Taking sail off a boat is not necessarily the best solution. In severe conditions it is possible to be undercanvased, particularly in short seas, where steering control may be vitally important. The technique chosen must suit conditions. A helmsman on watch is a good idea when manpower permits.

Heaving to

Advantages

The boat slows down and seems to 'stop', making only a little headway.

In general, little effort is required of the crew.

The boat assumes a 'natural' position, which often increases comfort on board.

Disadvantages

The boat makes considerable leeway.

There is a risk of being thrown beam-on to the seas.

Deckhouse, windows and hatches become vulnerable to wind and waves.

There is constant strain and chafe on sails and rigging.

Knock-downs and capsize may occur.

See: Heaving to

Running

Advantages

Maneuverability is maintained and the boat 'steered' through the seas.

If the direction of the storm is favorable, progress on course can be made.

Strain and chafe on sails and rigging is minimized.

Disadvantages

A danger exists of being pooped, that is, having a following sea break over the stern.

Another danger is broaching – being thrown inadvertently beam-on to the seas.

In high waves, conceivably the boat could be pitch-poled – turned end over end.

Plenty of sea room is required.

Someone must always be at the helm.

The most vulnerable parts of the boat – the cockpit and aft bulkhead – are exposed to the seas.

See: Running

NOTE:

Beyond a certain point there can be no prescriptions. Variables such as sea state, wind force, hull design, strength of the crew, position, weather forecast, etc., must be judged and weighed against the range of alternatives. Ultimately, each skipper must fall back on his own independent judgment.

If in doubt about whether to stay out to sea or run for harbor, stay out to sea.

Heliograph

A makeshift heliograph ■ 169

Materials

A glass mirror. Failing that, any shiny piece of bright metal, such as the lid of a ration tin, beer can, or tobacco tin.

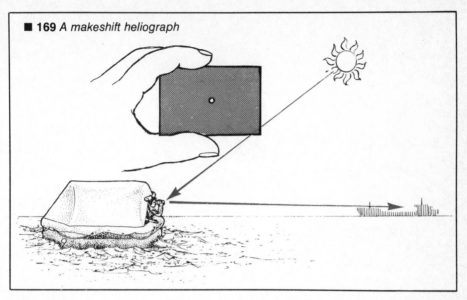

■ **169** *A makeshift heliograph*

Procedure

Punch a hole in the middle of the tin. With glass mirrors scrape away a bit of the silvering.

Hold the mirror or piece of tin a few inches from your face and sight the ship or aircraft through the hole.

Take your eye from the hole.

The sun's rays will pass through the hole onto your face or clothing.

Tilt the mirror or piece of tin until the reflection on your face or clothing disappears through the hole. At that point the sun will be reflected on the target.

Don't worry about flashing the mirror or piece of tin as you will do this inadvertently.

NOTE:

Heliograph signals can often be seen 10 miles away. For the man in the liferaft or disabled boat, this means his signal might be seen by a rescue vessel or aircraft before he can see them. Thus, he should begin signaling as soon as he hears the sound of motors and can detect its direction.

Help!

See also: Distress signals

International Code of Signals

'V'

VICTOR

'I REQUIRE ASSISTANCE.'

White

Red

■ **170**

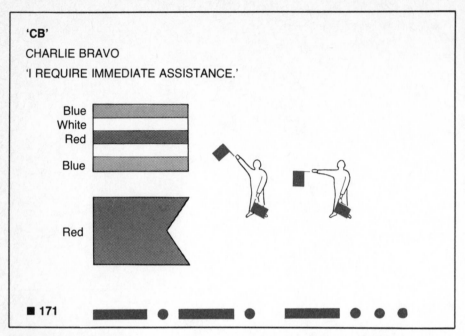

'CB'

CHARLIE BRAVO

'I REQUIRE IMMEDIATE ASSISTANCE.'

Blue
White
Red

Blue

Red

■ 171

Radiotelephone signal

When requiring immediate assistance, but *not* in distress, the prefix 'PAN PAN PAN' should be used instead of 'MAYDAY!'

Hemorrhages

See: Page 103

Holes

Immediate action

You must act immediately

By using damage control gear ■ 172.

or

Stuffing the hole with cushions, sail bags, blankets or mattresses (inflate the jackets when they are in place).

Clearing the area around the hole.

Backing the stuffing with wood – floorboards, tables, whatever is handy and malleable.

If the hole is on or near the waterline

Sail on the most favorable tack.

Heel the boat by shifting internal ballast, laying out the anchor chain, or running out a weighted boom.

Can the boat's pumping capacity cope with the inflow of water?

To estimate the boat's pumping capacity

Type of pump	Liters per minute
Manual	45–110 (12–30 gal.)
Electrical	45–110 (12–30 gal.)
Engine cooling	20–90 (5–28 gal.)
Engine driven	450–2,000 (140–500 gal.)

■ 172 *Damage control gear*

To estimate the inflow of water

For a three-fingered sized hole	Liters per minute
Near the waterline	300 (80 gal.)
4ft. (1m.) below the waterline	500 (130 gal.)
For a fist-sized hole	
Near the waterline	600 (160 gal.)
4ft. (1m.) below the waterline	1,200 (315 gal.)

Temporary repair

METHOD 1   Collision mat ■ 173

This can be manufactured quickly from a piece of canvas roughly 4ft. (1m.) on a side, a weight or length of chain, and some line.

By adjusting the lines you can position the mat virtually anywhere on the hull. However, they must be kept taut, for if the mat is sucked into the hole it can easily be ripped.

The mat will make a tighter seal if it is backed with carpet or a layer of foam rubber. This can be cut from a mattress and stitched to the canvas. **See also: Leaks**

NOTE:

A small tarpaulin with reinforced grommets at the corners makes a handy collision mat. It can also be used as an awning, a rain-water catcher, and a dodger and is worth carrying aboard.

■ **173** *Positioning a collision mat*

A sail as a collision mat

■ **174**

■ **175**

METHOD 2   A sail as collision mat
■ **174, 175**

A stormsail is preferable, and failing that a small jib.

Set the sail in place from the bow.

Make the tack and clew fast to a fitting fore and aft so that the foot is above the waterline ■ **174.**

Attach a rope to the head, and pass it under the bow.

Pull the head beneath the bow, then using the head and clew lines work the sail into position ■ **175.**

Keep the lines taut at all times.

METHOD 3   Cement

Mix one part cement with one part plaster.

Take an equal part of clay or dirt and add water until it becomes a runny mud.

Work the mud into the plaster cement to form a putty.

Use immediately as the putty will begin to harden in a few minutes.

Apply the patch from outside the hull against a backing plate.

For other means of repair **See: Fiberglass repair, Aluminum repair, Wood repair, Steel hull repair, Ferrocement repair**

Hull patches

See: Holes

Hurricanes

See: Law of storms

I

Ice

See: Water

Immersion foot

See also: Exposure

Symptoms

Legs or feet seem to 'fall asleep' to the point of insensitivity.

Swelling.

Toes become stiff.

Touch produces severe pain.

Treatment

Warm the feet or legs *slowly. Do not immerse in water!*

Wrap the feet or legs in rags or blankets which are at a moderate (warm) temperature.

Gradually warm the legs, moving from the body downwards, but do *not* rub or massage as this will damage the tissue.

Elevate the legs on soft cushions or pillows.

If infection develops, use antibiotics. **See: Antibiotics**

Do not walk until condition has improved.

Infection

Local infection

Symptoms

Part is red, hot, and tender.

Treatment

Localized collections of pus should be drained.

If necessary, take antibiotics. **See: Antibiotics**

Systemic infection, such as, pneumonia, septicemia and strep throat.

Symptoms

Fatigue

Loss of appetite.

General aches and pains.

Headache.

Temperature.

Increased pulse rate.

Perspiration.

NOTE:

Infections often arrive without warning and the symptoms appear rapidly.

Treatment

Rest.

Antibiotics. **See: Antibiotics**

Injections

For intramuscular injections ■ 176, 177, 178, 179

The target is the upper, outer quadrant of the buttocks.

Clean the area with alcohol ■ **176.**

Break the top of the ampul.

Insert the needle and fill the syringe by pulling out the plunger ■ **177.**

Then, hold it needle up and empty any remaining air by squeezing out a few drops of liquid ■ **178.**

With one hand squeeze a fold of flesh, and with the other hold the syringe like a pencil and jab it fast and forcefully on the target ■ **179.**

Release the fold and slowly squeeze out the contents of the syringe.

Quickly remove the syringe and cover the spot with a bit of cotton wool.

■ **176** *The target for an intramuscular injection*

Preparing the syringe

■ 177

■ 178

■ 179

International code of signals

See: Anchoring, Danger, Disabled, Distress signals, Fire, Help!, Man overboard!, Medical assistance, Pilot, Stop, Towing

J

Jackstay

See: Safety harness

Jury-rigging

Temporary masts ■ 180, 181

Additional height can be had from the boom, spinnaker pole ■ **180A**, an oar, or bits of the old mast lashed to the stump ■ **180B.**

If the mast was stepped on the keel, the stump can be removed and the broken mast restepped.

If the mast is aluminum, often a section of the old mast can be lowered into the stump, wedged in with battens or floorboards, and lashed in place with wire or rope. If the break is high, trim down the stump before inserting the mast ■ **181.**

Temporary shrouds and stays ■ 182, 183

Cable can be salvaged from the broken rigging, especially the upper shrouds which are longer, lifelines or the wire luff of sails.

Bend one end into a large strop, secured by wire rope clips. **See: Bulldog clamps (wire rope clips)**

Pass the strop over the spreader or hounds ■ **182**, and fasten the other end to a deck fitting by a lashing, turnbuckle or Spanish windlass. **See: Lanyards, Spanish windlass**

■ **182** *Jury-rigged shrouds*

■ **183** *Jury-rigged shrouds*

Jury-rigged masts

■ **180**

■ **181**

Temporary and movable crosstrees ■ 184

A spar or oar is loosely lashed at the foot of the mast and allowed to lean to windward.

A line from the masthead is tied to the end.

When in position – athwartships – the spar is guyed fore and aft.

When changing tacks, the entire system must be moved to the other side.

■ **184** *Temporary crosstrees*

■ 185 *Raising a jury-mast*

Raising a jury-mast ■ 185

Bouse the foot of the broken mast to any available deck fitting, the mast stump or tabernacle ■ 185D.

Loosely rig the backstay.

Attach lengths of line to the upper shrouds on both sides. Run the lines through blocks ■ 185E at deck level and back to the cockpit winches ■ 185B.

Rig a pair of sheer legs or a dead man ■ 185A and brace it against the coachroof or a deck fitting ■ 185C.

Attach the forestay to the upper end of the dead man ■ 185A and a block and tackle from there to a fitting on the bow.

While hoisting the mast with the block and tackle from the bow, steady it with the cockpit winches.

Temporary halyards ■ 186

Shackles and blocks can be lashed to the top of the broken mast as high as possible. It may be necessary to notch the mast, or dent it with a hammer to prevent the lashing from sliding.

■ 186 *Temporary halyards*

Sail plans

In general – set as much sail as possible. Make the maximum use of smaller sails – jibs, storm-jibs and mizzens. If necessary a larger sail can be made smaller by simply knotting it.

See: Spanish reef ■ 187.

■ 187 *A Spanish reef*

Sloops and cutters

METHOD 1

Remove the boom, and turn the jib 90 degrees, or use a trysail as a loose-footed mainsail. A storm-jib or knotted jib becomes the foresail ■ 188.

■ 188 *The jib as a loose-footed mainsail*

METHOD 2

Remove the boom and lash it to the mast as a topmast. A reefed mainsail is rigged loose-footed ■ 189.

■ 189 *A loose-footed mainsail and the boom as a topmast*

METHOD 3

An oar or spinnaker pole is lashed at an angle to the mast stump, or if the mast is stepped in a tabernacle, the stump is canted aft. A single jib or genoa, upside down, is hoisted lateen style ■ 190.

■ 190 *A genoa hoisted lateen style*

METHOD 4

A light, sprit boom is lashed to the old boom fitting. The spritsail is fabricated by removing the hanks from two jibs and joining them together with a tight lacing ■ 191.

■ 191 *A makeshift spritsail*

Two-masted rigs

If the mizzen mast is still secure

METHOD 1

A mizzen staysail, jib or genoa, turned 90 degrees, is hoisted as a foresail ■ 192.

■ 192 *The jib on its side*

METHOD 2

A temporary foremast is rigged. The storm-jib becomes the foresail, and the jib or mizzen staysail is hoisted as a mizzen staysail ■ 193.

■ 193 *The jib as a mizzen staysail*

Jury rudders

A makeshift rudder using a sweep ■ 194, 195

Materials ■ 194

The shaft can be made from a boom, reinforced oars or the spinnaker pole.

The blade can be constructed from floorboards, or locker doors lashed or through-bolted to the shaft.

Procedure

The sweep is lashed to the stern, either to the stern pulpit, a stanchion, deck fitting, an 'X'-shaped crutch or, if necessary, a 'V' cut into the transom.

NOTE:

It is important to keep the turning point of the sweep as low as possible.

To prevent the oar from floating on the surface:

A small block and tackle is tied from the

■ 194

■ 195 *A makeshift rudder using a sweep*

handle to a wire rope clip fixed to the backstay.

Weights, such as shackles or lengths of chain, are attached to the underside of the blade.

To obtain more leverage, and thus permit easier steering, a spar or oar can be lashed across the stern and blocks secured to the ends. The steering lines run from the blade, through the blocks to the cockpit winches ■ **196.**

To steer

Blocks and tackles can be tied to the inboard end of the sweep and secured port and starboard to the mizzen shrouds, deck fittings or stanchions ■ **197.**

Lines from the blade can be run through

■ 196 *A makeshift rudder using a sweep and a spar for leverage*

blocks lashed on the stern and then to the cockpit winches.

If the boat has a stern pulpit, the spar should be lashed to the railing to give further support to the sweep which slides along it ■ **198.**

NOTE:

Many boats can be steered quite well on a wide range of courses using the sails and leaving the leeline free. It might take less time and effort to do this than to rig a jury rudder.

■ **197** *A makeshift rudder using a sweep with blocks and tackles for steering*

■ **198** *A makeshift rudder using a sweep with a spar for support*

A makeshift rudder, particularly for double-enders and counter sterns with nearly straight transoms ■ **199**

■ **199** *A makeshift rudder for double-enders and counter sterns*

Materials

The blade is fabricated from reinforced floorboards, bulkheads, locker doors or hatch covers.

The hinges are two eye bolts and two shackles.

The metal reinforcing is cut from a pot.

The tiller is any spare piece of wood.

Procedure

Drill two holes for the eye bolts in the transom, or for double-enders, left or right of the stern post.

Prepare the rudder itself and nail or screw on the metal reinforcing.

Connect the shackles to the eye bolts.

Pass the bolt ends of the eye bolts through the holes and securely bolt them in place.

A makeshift rudder, particularly for boats with stern pulpits ■ 200, 201, 202, 203, 204

Materials

The blade is fabricated from reinforced floorboards, bulkheads, locker doors or hatch covers ■ 200.

The shaft is a spar, section of the pulpit or a stanchion.

The tiller is cut from spare wood ■ 201.

The sheave is cut from a length of pipe or strong plastic hose ■ 203.

A makeshift rudder for boats with stern pulpits and counter sterns

■ 201

■ 200

■ 202

Procedure

The sheave is lashed in place ■ **203.**

The rudder and shaft are run through it.

Supporting lines from the blade are run forward and secured to stanchions or deck fittings ■ **204.**

A tiller ■ **201** or a yoke and lines ■ **202** are used for steering.

A makeshift rudder for boats with stern pulpits and counter sterns

■ **203**

■ **204**

A makeshift rudder for boats without stern pulpits ■ 205

Procedure

The rudder can be lashed to a stern quarter.

A strong spar athwartships ■ **205A** is lashed to the cockpit winches, the coachroof, deck fittings or stanchions.

The sheave or rudder shaft is secured by a lashing to the spar ■ **205B.**

Supporting lines from the blade and the shaft are run fore and aft ■ **205C.**

NOTE:

It is preferable to lash the rudder on the leeward side so that the blade will be deeper in the water.

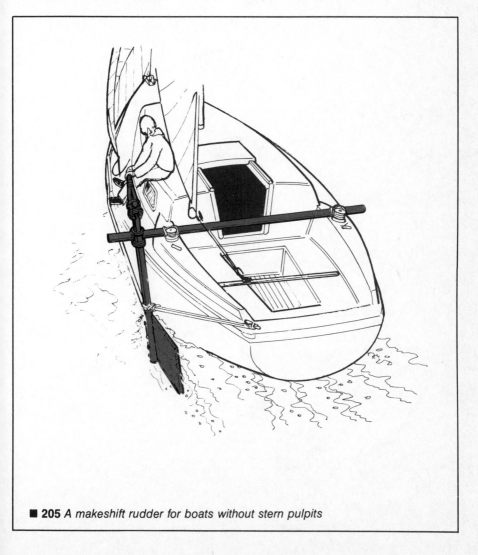

■ **205** *A makeshift rudder for boats without stern pulpits*

A makeshift rudder using a drogue ■ 206

Materials

The drogue can be a car tire, sail bag full of rags, a jib or a small sea anchor.

A length of strong line.

A strong spar.

Procedure

The drogue is towed at least one full wavelength behind the boat.

The steering lines are tied to the warp with rolling hitches about 10–17ft. (3–5 meters) off the stern.

A strong spar is lashed athwartships on the stern, and blocks attached to either end.

The steering lines pass through the blocks and on to the cockpit winches.

■ 206 *A makeshift rudder using a drogue*

■ **207** *A makeshift rudder using a plank*

A makeshift rudder using a plank ■ 207

Procedure

Lash a spar, boom, or strong length of timber in place as a boomkin ■ **207A.**

NOTE:

In emergency conditions, the boom should be regarded as an available spar since the mainsail can always be rigged loose-footed. **See: Jury-rigging**

Tie a weight, such as a length of chain or a small anchor to the end of the plank ■ **207B.**

Lash one end securely to the stern pulpit ■ **207C.**

By means of a block and tackle, or just a block, attach the other end of the plank to the boomkin ■ **207D.** Run the line to the cockpit to control the angle of the blade ■ **207F.**

The steering lines are run from the end of the plank forward to blocks and then on to the cockpit winches ■ **207E.**

A makeshift rudder using the jib boom or spinnaker pole
■ 208, 209

Procedure

Lash a spar, boom or a strong length of timber in place as a boomkin ■ **208A, 209A.**

A section of floorboard or plank is lashed or bolted to one end of the jib boom (or spinnaker pole) as a blade ■ **208B, 209B** and weighted with chain ■ **208C, 209C.**

Pass an eye bolt through the rudder fitting and bolt it in place ■ **208D, 209D.**

The boom or pole fitting is clipped onto the eye bolt.

The boom is supported by means of a line to a block attached to the end of the boomkin ■ **208E, 209E.**

Steering lines are run forward to blocks and then onto cockpit winches ■ **208F, 209F.**

■ **208** *A makeshift rudder using a spinnaker pole*

■ **209** *A makeshift rudder using a spinnaker pole*

Jury steering

See: Tiller

K

Kedging off

See: Aground

Knots

Anchor bend ■ 210

To connect a warp with a ring or anchor.

Bowline ■ 211

Wherever a bight is needed.

See: Bowline – for a one-handed method.

■ 210

■ 211

Carrick bend ■ 212

To join heavy warps or lines of unequal size.

NOTE:

The ends can be tucked either over or under several times or bound to the line.

Sheet bend ■ 213

To join a line to a bight or two lines of unequal size.

When joining two lines an extra turn should be taken making the knot into a double sheet bend.

Stopper knot or rolling hitch ■ 214

To make a line fast to a shroud, stay or spar which will not slip when pulled.

■ 212

■ 214

■ 213

Tugboat hitch ■ 215

To attach a warp to a samson post or bollard.

■ 215

L

Landfall signs

Birds

The presence of birds cannot be taken as an indication that land is near. However, flight direction in the early evening is often a good indication of the bearing of land.

Breeze

Usually, a breeze comes from the land in the morning, and blows toward the land in the evening.

Clouds

Cumulus clouds

If they appear to be stationary in a clear sky or if other clouds are moving rapidly, there is probably land or an island.

A line of cumulus clouds

Often this will appear over and along a coastline.

A greenish-blue tint on the underside of the clouds

Occasionally, a flat cloud base may act as a mirror and reflect the green of a tropical island or a lagoon. This occurs most often in low latitudes.

A light tint on the underside of the clouds

This may be a reflection of an ice-field or snow-covered land.

Surf

This can usually be heard long before it can be seen.

Color of water

In general, the lighter the color, the shallower the depth.

Smells

Those such as burning wood, swamps, and pollution often carry long distances, especially after a rain.

Winged insects

These do indicate the presence of land.

Landing signals

Landing signals for small boats made from shoreward or ashore

'THIS IS THE BEST PLACE TO LAND.'

By day

Vertical motion of a white flag.

Vertical motions of the arms.

A green star signal.

'K' − · − transmitted by either light or sound.

By night

Vertical motion of a white flare or light.

A green star signal.

'K' − · − transmitted by either light or sound.

'LANDING HERE IS HIGHLY DANGEROUS.'

By day

Horizontal motion of a white flag.

Horizontal motions of the arms.

A red star signal.

'S' · · · transmitted by either light or sound.

By night

Horizontal motion of a white flare or light.

A red star signal.

'S' · · · transmitted by either light or sound.

'LANDING HERE IS HIGHLY DANGEROUS. A MORE FAVORABLE PLACE TO LAND IS IN THE DIRECTION INDICATED.'

By day

Horizontal motion of a white flag, followed by placing the flag in the ground and carrying another flag in the direction indicated.

By day or night

Horizontal motion of a white light or flare, followed by placing the light or flare on the ground and carrying another white light or flare in the direction to be indicated.

Firing a red star signal vertically, and a white star in the *direction of a better landing place*.

'S' · · · followed by 'R' · – · if the better landing is to the *right of the approach line*.

'S' · · · followed by 'L' · – ·· if the better landing is to the *left of the approach line*.

Lanyards

Lanyards can be used to replace broken turnbuckles, repair lifelines and set up damaged standing rigging. Six to eight turns of ⅛-inch Dacron line will equal the strength of small-craft wire cable.

To form an eye on the end of a piece of broken wire cable **See: Wire rope clips**

For rigging failures ■ 216, 217

■ 216   ■ 217

For lifelines or lashings with a pull in only one direction ■ 218

■ 218

Lashings

Lashing two spars together ■ 219, 220

Begin with a clove hitch.

Tuck the short end under the long one as you make the first turn.

Make at least two complete turns, pulling the line taut after each one.

To make it really tight, add frapping turns (at right angles) to lashing, passing between the spars.

End with a clove hitch or two half hitches.

NOTE:

Whether lashing two spars together or at right angles to each other, the method is the same.

■ 219   ■ 220

Latitude

See: Sextant – A Sun Sight without a sextant (page 206); **Sight Reduction Tables** – Latitude without Sight Reduction Tables – a 'Noon Sight' (page 212)

Law of storms

See also: Heavy weather

General indications of an approaching revolving storm

Cirrus and cirrostratus clouds.

Increasing humidity.

Sudden puffs of hot or cold wind.

A red, copper-colored sky at sunrise and/or sunset.

An unsteady or falling barometer.

A heavy, unaccountable swell.

Unusual behavior in sea birds.

One's position relative to the storm ■ 221

In the northern hemisphere

When an observer faces the wind – the storm's center is approximately 110 degrees to his right.

Then:

If the wind veers to the right, he is in the right-hand semicircle, that is, the center of the storm will pass to his right.

If the wind moves ι, the left and backs, he is in the left-hand semicircle, that is, the center of the storm will pass to his left.

If the wind is constant in direction, but increasing in force, he is directly in the path of the storm or directly behind it.

If the wind has an easterly component, the storm is approaching; if westerly, it has passed.

If the barometer falls – he is in front of the storm center.

If the barometer rises, he is behind the storm center.

In the northern hemisphere, the most dangerous semicircle is to the right of the path of the storm.

NOTE:

In the southern hemisphere all directions are the reverse.

If in the direct path of the storm

Run with the wind on the starboard quarter. **See: Running**

If in the right-hand semicircle

Heave-to on the starboard tack. **See: Heaving-to**

If in the left-hand semicircle

Run with the wind on the starboard quarter. **See: Running**

Leaks

A checklist for leaks

Seacocks: galley, toilet, engine intake and exhaust, bilge pumps

Both propeller shaft and rudder post

Throughhull fittings

Stuffing box

Water tank

The hull: along the stem, garboards, transom, hull-deck connections, keel

Quick repair

Caulk with: caulking cotton, greased rags, underwater epoxy, bandages, foam rubber, plugs and towels.

Repairs

See: Fiberglass, Wood repair, Aluminum repair, Steel hull repair, Ferrocement repair

For emergency repair of holes **See: Holes**

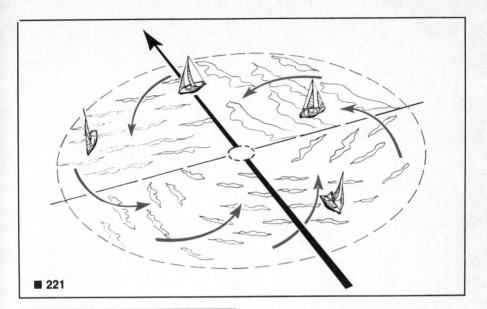

■ 221

Lee shore

Getting underway from a lee shore under sail ■ 222

With a dinghy, lay out a second anchor off the bow and tie the warp to the stern ■ **222A. See: Anchoring**

Hoist the sails but do *not* sheet them in.

Haul in the stern warp until the boat is beam on to the wind ■ **222B.**

Raise the bow anchor.

Let go and buoy the stern warp ■ **222C.**

Sheet in the sails and sail away close-hauled ■ **222D.**

For anchoring on a lee shore **See: Anchoring**

■ 222 *Getting underway from a lee shore under sail*

Liferaft

Launching ■ 223

Tie the liferaft painter to a secure point, for example, a stanchion or the lifeline.

Throw the entire container or valise overboard.

Pull the painter to inflate the raft.

Full inflation should occur within a minute.

Board the raft, *then* cut the painter.

If the raft cannot be brought alongside, jump directly onto the raft. **See: Abandon ship!**

NOTE:

Do *not* remove wet clothing, as even that provides some insulation and shelter from the elements.

■ **223** *Launching a liferaft*

Getting the injured aboard ■ 224, 225

Once alongside the raft, turn the injured man so that his back faces the raft's door.

Grasp him under the armpits.

Push him *down* into the water ■ **224.**

The buoyancy of his body and the lifejacket he should be wearing will thrust him upwards so he can easily be pulled on board ■ **225.**

■ **224** *Getting the injured aboard*

225 *Getting the injured aboard*

NOTE:

To reach someone injured, motionless, or who can't swim, don't leave the liferaft. Instead, pull in the drogue, roll it into a ball, throw it in the direction of the survivor and pull the liferaft to him.

Heavy weather

A sea anchor or drogue should be streamed to hold the raft up to the wind and waves. Often its effectiveness can be improved by adding a riding weight.

Some castaways report that in high seas, *deflating* the raft slightly can be advantageous. It allows the raft to shape itself to the waves, rather than present a rigid and vulnerable profile. **See: Sea anchor**

Capsize ■ 226

A cloth loop and the gas cylinder are usually found on the bottom of most rafts. Using these a swimmer can climb onto the overturned raft. He should attempt to point the raft into the wind, wait for the right wave, then lean backwards and pull the raft upright.

If there is no handhold on the bottom of the raft, the painter can be carried across the underside and used as a lever.

■ **226** *Righting an overturned liferaft*

Repairs

Clamp repair procedure ■ 227, 228, 229

Dip plug in water to make the insertion easier.

Push the bottom plate through the hole in the fabric. If the hole is too small, enlarge it carefully so the plate can just be forced in ■ 227.

Pull the bottom plate back against the inner fabric surface and screw down the top plate against the outer fabric surface ■ 228.

Hold the loose edges in place while adjusting the clamp to cover the hole completely.

Screw down the wing nut firmly ■ 229.

Patches

Dry and clean the surface where the patch is to be applied.

Select a patch large enough to have a safety margin of at least one inch all round the hole.

Roughen the surface of the area to be patched.

Apply cement to both the patch and the area round the hole. Allow to dry, then apply a second coat and a third.

When the cement becomes tacky, press the patch on evenly and securely.

If possible do not inflate the raft hard until the patch has had 24 hours to dry.

Plugs

These are generally used for larger holes.

The fabric is drawn around the plug and securely bound with cord to make an airtight seal.

NOTE:

Nearly all liferafts are designed to withstand a *minimum* of 30 days at sea in the worst of conditions. A great deal of wear comes from the flexing of the fabric; for this reason the chambers should be kept as rigid as possible.

■ **227, 228, 229** *Clamp repair procedure*

Strategy

Wait for help to arrive?

or

Begin sailing toward the nearest shore?

Circumstances should dictate this decision. Where they don't, the gambler's choice is to make sail.

Besides the psychological boost of 'doing something' instead of just 'waiting around', often the closer one is to land the more traffic there is at sea.

Judging from the experience of recent castaways, such as the Robertsons and the Baileys, the sooner a castaway accepts the fact that he is on his own, the better. Even with the best emergency radio gear, flares, and radar reflectors, equipment can malfunction, freighters be piloted by sleepy watches and radar scanners rotate only for regulations. Numerous ships passed close to the Robertsons and the Baileys before they were finally rescued. Viewing the liferaft as a sailing boat may well be the only means to survival.

Take the EPIRB with you in the raft.

If a distress signal has been broadcast, a reasonable length of time to wait for help is five days. After that time the statistical chances of rescue fall off dramatically.

If land is in sight

There is usually an on-shore wind in the mornings, and often in the afternoons as well. In those conditions the sea anchor should be streamed only at night.

If land is not in sight

See: Landfall signs

Progress can *only* be made to leeward.

When the wind is unfavorable, a sea anchor should be streamed to 'park' the raft.

Progress can be made, depending on wind conditions, up to as much as 40 miles a day. This can be achieved by either hoisting a makeshift sail or holding the raft's entry port into the wind by means of a half-tripped sea anchor
■ 230.

■ **230** *Making way with a liferaft*

Food from the sea

Fish

Do *not* eat fish that have spines or bristles instead of scales. **See: Fishing**

Do *not* eat fish which puff themselves up into a ball.

Do *not* eat fish which are pallid at the gills.

Do *not* eat fish which have been left in the sun for more than two hours.

Do *not* eat shark livers.

Do eat the heart, liver and brains of fish as often they are more nourishing than the flesh.

Eat fish only if fresh water is available. Fish are salty and the digestive process draws more on the body's supply of water than other types of food.

For fishing methods and preserving **See: Fishing**

Barnacles and shellfish

Barnacles will often grow on the underside of the raft or on trailing lines. All are edible, *except* if they have lived on surfaces coated with antifouling.

Crabmeat is edible except for the loose, finger-like spongy material around the edge of a deshelled crab, and the stomach, which is just below the head.

Birds ■ 231, 232, 233, 234, 235, 236

All sea birds are edible.

They can be caught with fishhooks, baited with small pieces of wood or metal, or caught by hand. When trying to seize one by hand, wait until the bird has settled and folded its wings.

Birds should be skinned rather than plucked.

Provided fresh water which aids digestion has been drunk that day, drink the bird's blood.

Eat the entrails first, as the meat may be dried and preserved.

Turtles

They are best caught by their flippers, hauled into the raft and killed while on their back. Thrust a knife into the neck in order to cut the veins and arteries on both sides.

Drink the blood immediately before it coagulates. The meat can be cut in strips, eaten straight away or dried.

Plankton and seaweed

These can be caught by trailing a fine-weave net. However, they should be washed in *fresh* water before being eaten, as some varieties are *toxic*. Eat them only as a last resort.

Water

Drink as much as you can before boarding the liferaft.

In the raft, do not drink for the first 24 hours.

Do *not* drink sea water. The body can tolerate only a small amount, as the salt content of sea water is three times more than the body can cope with. Also, do not mix salt water with fresh water.

NOTE:

In moderate conditions a person can survive five or six days without water and not suffer any permanent body damage.

Do not eat unless you have some water to drink. The digestive process consumes body fluid.

If possible, drink your water ration in small quantities at several times during the day.

Collect any morning dew from the cold surfaces of the raft.

Since most body water is lost through perspiration, keeping the body cool by clothing soaked in sea water is a vital means of conservation.

See: Rainwater, Solar still, Water

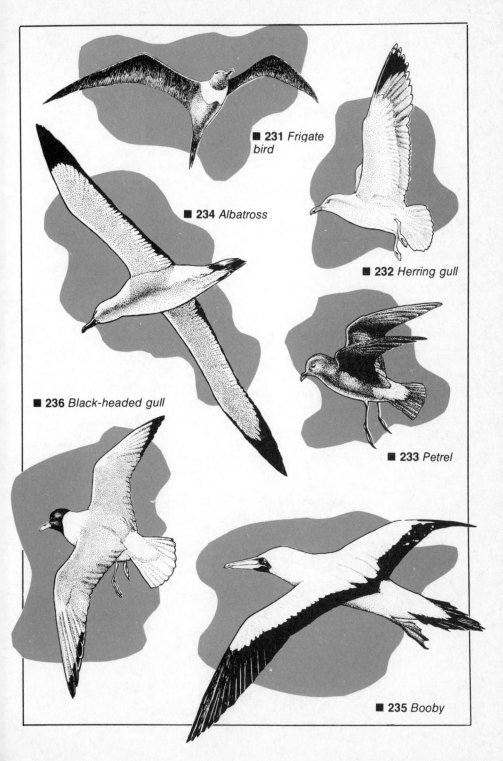

■ **231** *Frigate bird*

■ **234** *Albatross*

■ **232** *Herring gull*

■ **236** *Black-headed gull*

■ **233** *Petrel*

■ **235** *Booby*

■ **237** *Landing a liferaft in a heavy swell*

Landing ■ 237

If possible, do not land with on-shore wind *and* waves.

Stream a sea anchor, and prepare an emergency one.

Cut away the canopy so that no one will be trapped inside should the raft pitchpole.

Persons should be fully clothed, wearing lifejackets, oilskins and whatever else is available for protection against rocks or coral.

When near the surf, all occupants should move toward the seaward side to maintain the raft's stability.

If the surf is extremely heavy, the raft may need to be flooded in order for it to remain stable.

Should the raft capsize, stay with it as long as possible.

WARNING:

Always attempt to land on the lee side of coral islands or atolls.

Attempt to land only at high tide when the waves may pass over the reef without breaking.

Do not attempt a landing at night.

■ **238** *The dinghy as a liferaft*

The dinghy as a liferaft ■ 238, 239, 240

■ **239** *The dinghy as a liferaft*

Materials

A bucket, which will serve as a storage container, bailer and drogue.

A canopy against exposure: preferably Day-Glo in color, it should have a large entrance opening at one end and a smaller port at the other to control the drogue. The canopy can be drawn over the dinghy like a sausage skin and tied in place.

Wooden or aluminum struts to hold the canopy erect.

Shock cords to lash emergency flotation in place.

Flotation: inner tubes, expanded polystyrene packing, cushions, empty bottles, spare lifejackets, fenders. A normal-sized tubular fender will have about 55–65lb. (25–30kg.) of positive buoyancy, and the yacht's supply, if securely lashed in place, can make a small dinghy unsinkable.

NOTE:

If the dinghy is an inflatable it should be left on deck half-inflated during a passage.

■ **240** *The dinghy as a liferaft*

Lightning storms

In severe electrical storms

The crew should go below.

The helmsman should avoid any contact with a metal part of the boat.

Lightning, like most natural phenomena, is not totally predictable. But as a general rule: it will strike the top of the mast. From there it will take the shortest path, via metal, to the water. Should there be a gap in this circuit the lightning bolt will burn its way through. Metal objects within 7ft. (2 meters) from this path are susceptible to side flashes.

Steel hulls

The rigging and hull act as a conductor, provided the shrouds are well connected (in an electrical sense) to the hull.

Wood and GRP hulls

The most likely place to find a break in the circuit is between the chain plates of the upper shrouds and the water.

Temporary protection

A piece of thick cable, preferably copper, can be bonded to the base of the upper shrouds and the other end dropped in the water. If possible, a piece of screen or thin metal plate should be attached to the end to help diffuse the electricity.

or

A length of chain can be well bonded to the shrouds and dropped in the water.

Lightning protection ■ 241

It is quite *unlikely* that a yacht will be struck by lightning, and if so, that she will be damaged.

Nonetheless, a lightning rod (conductor), at least 6in. (15cm.) long, should be mounted on top of the mast, particularly if the mast is wooden. All other metallic instruments, anemometers, radio aerials, etc., should be grounded to the rod to prevent side flashes.

This rod, if properly grounded, will provide the boat with a 'protective cone', the sides of which will be at an angle of about 60 degrees from the mast.

At the other end, on nonmetallic boats, a copper strip should be connected between the chain plates on both sides and the keel bolts. If there is no external ballast, a small copper plate should be fixed to the outside of the hull and the cable connected to it. One shouldn't worry about grounding the forestay or the backstay as the circuit via the shrouds will nearly always be shorter.

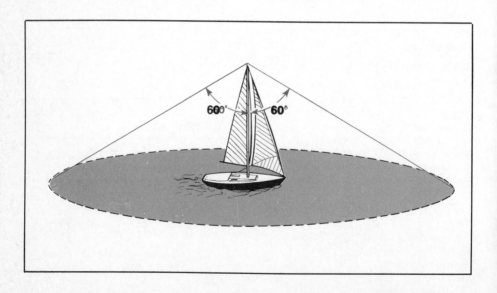

Lights

Power vessels

Underway: masthead light forward, sidelights and a stern light.

If over 170ft. (50 meters): a second masthead light abaft and higher than the forward one ■ **242.**

NOTE

These regulations conform to the international rules of the road and differ is some regards from the rules for inland waterways.

A vessel constrained by her draft

For instance a supertanker: three red lights in addition to her normal steaming lights ■ **243.**

■ **242** *A power vessel underway*

■ **243** *A vessel restricted in maneuverability*

Fishing vessels (over 170ft., or 50 meters)

Trawling: white all-round light aft and green over white lights forward ■ **244.**

Trawling in pairs: searchlight forward and in the direction of the other pair ■ **245.**

■ **244** *A fishing vessel engaged in trawling*

■ **245** *Fishing boats trawling in pairs*

■ **246** *A fishing boat engaged in fishing*

Fishing vessels over 70ft. (20 meters) but not engaged in trawling: red over white lights ■ **246.**

Hovercraft

Flashing yellow light (120 flashes per minute) ■ 247.

■ 247 Hovercraft

Pilot ship on duty

At anchor white over red near the masthead ■ 248.

■ 248 A pilot ship at anchor

Vessel aground

Two red lights ■ 249.

■ 249 A vessel aground

For light patterns of ships at anchor **See: Anchoring**

For light patterns of ships under tow **See: Towing**

Lighthouse characteristics

Fixed (F.): a continuous steady light.

Flashing (Fl.): single flash at regular intervals. Duration of light always less than the period of darkness.

Group Flashing (Gp.Fl.): two or more brilliant flashes in succession at regular intervals.

Isophase (Iso.): duration of light and darkness are equal.

Occulting (Occ.): steady light with total eclipse at regular intervals. Duration of darkness less than that of light.

Quick Flashing (Qk.Fl.): continuous flash at rate of 50 or 60 per minute.

Group Occulting (Gp.Occ.): two or more eclipses in a group at regular intervals.

Alternating (Alt.): a light which alters in color in successive flashes or eclipses.

Lloyd's of London

Reporting through Lloyd's

At sea any ship may be asked to report a yacht to Lloyd's of London. The international code signal is 'ZD2'.

The ship will send a telegram to Lloyd's giving the name of the yacht, its position, and any other message. The cost of the service is paid by the owner of the yacht, hence arrangements with Lloyd's should be made before a passage.

■ 250 Reporting through Lloyd's of London

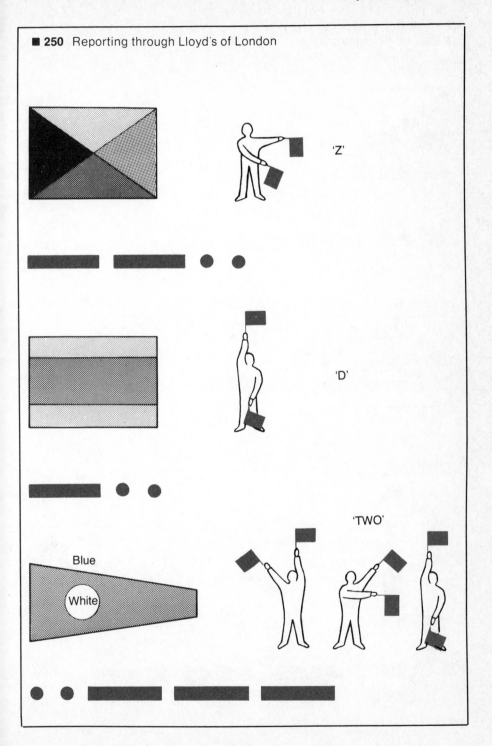

■ **250** Reporting through the United States Coast Guard

'Z'

'D'

'ONE'

White

Red

Reporting through the United States Coast Guard

To report to the U.S. Coast Guard in New York the signal is 'ZD1'.

Log

An emergency log ■ 251

Materials

A kitchen or fuel-oil funnel.

Elastic bands.

170ft. (50 meters) of line.

A watch.

Procedure

One end of the line is tied to the small end of the funnel.

Elastic bands form a harness to the funnel's large end and are lashed to the line.

Two knots are tied exactly 100ft. (30.5 meters) apart.

The funnel is thrown overboard and the line runs out freely.

When the first knot passes through your hand, timing begins, and ends when the second knot appears.

Seconds	Knots
120	= $\frac{1}{2}$
60	= 1
30	= 2
20	= 3
15	= 4
12	= 5
10	= 6

To pull in the log, a quick tug on the line will stretch the elastic bands and pitchpole the funnel.

■ 251 *An emergency log*

Speed from distance

If distance traveled – from the log – is timed, the boat's speed can easily be calculated.

Time	Speed												
	2	3	4	5	6	7	8	9	10	11	12	13	14
0 h 05	0.2	0.2	0.3	0.4	0.5	0.6	0.7	0.7	0.8	0.9	1.0	1.1	1.2
0 h 10	0.3	0.5	0.7	0.8	1.0	1.2	1.3	1.5	1.7	1.8	2.0	2.2	2.3
0 h 15	0.5	0.7	1.0	1.2	1.5	1.7	2.0	2.2	2.5	2.7	3.0	3.2	3.5
0 h 20	0.7	1.0	1.3	1.7	2.0	2.3	2.7	3.0	3.3	3.7	4.0	4.3	4.7
0 h 25	0.8	1.2	1.7	2.1	2.5	2.9	3.3	3.7	4.2	4.6	5.0	5.4	5.8
0 h 30	1.0	1.5	2.0	2.5	3.0	3.5	4.0	4.5	5.0	5.5	6.0	6.5	7.0
0 h 45	1.5	2.2	3.0	3.7	4.5	5.2	6.0	6.7	7.5	8.2	9.0	9.7	10.5

Distance

Longitude

see: Sextant – Longitude without a sextant (page 206); A Sun Sight without a sextant (page 206); **Sight reduction tables** – Finding Longitude without Sight Reduction Tables (page 212)

Lost!

One is never lost in the full sense of the word, that is, cast on an unknown ocean without bearings or boundaries.

Some facts are always known, or at least can be approximated.

1 – A previous position, if only your starting point.

2 – The time since you left that point, even if it is no more than a reasonable guess.

3 – An estimation of maximum speed. If not your actual speed, at least the maximum possible speed, allowing for drift, tide and current.

Speed × *Time* = *Maximum Distance* traveled since your last known position. If that distance becomes the radius of a circle, your position *must* be somewhere within it ■ 252.

4 – An estimation of minimum speed, allowing for drift, tide and current. By multiplying this speed by Time, your minimum distance from your last known position is found. When this is plotted along the radius, the inner portion of the circle can be eliminated ■ 253.

Speed × Time = Maximum Distance Traveled   Last known position

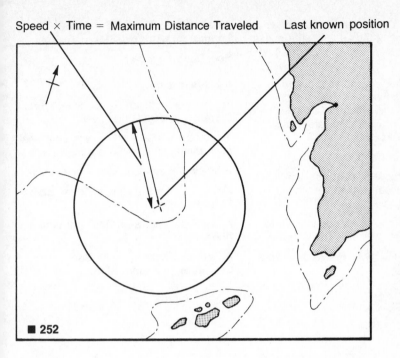

■ 252

Area of your possible position   Maximum Distance   Minimum Distance

■ 253

5 – If the boat's compass functions, your course, or, at the very least, a guess whose error would be no more than plus or minus 45 degrees.

Plotting that course as a radius eliminates three quadrants of the circle. Your position must be somewhere within the remaining section ■ 254.

Land is *not* in sight

To estimate more closely your position, additional navigational information is necessary:

A reading from an echo sounder. **See: Echo sounder**

An RDF bearing. **See: Radio direction finder**

An astronavigational sight. **See: Longitude, Latitude, Stars**

See: Landfall signs

Land is in sight

The distance-off can be estimated. **See: Distance at sea, Distance-off**

To establish an exact 'fix' some additional navigational information is necessary:

A bearing to an identifiable point ashore.

A reading from the echo sounder. **See: Echo sounder**

An RDF bearing. **See: Radio direction finder**

An astronavigational sight. **See: Longitude, Latitude, Stars**

Area of your possible position   Your estimated course

■ 254

■ **255** *Lying off by heaving to*

■ **256** *Lying off by sailing with the mainsail*

Lying off

When waiting for dawn, port signals, a tide change, or a pilot it may be necessary to 'stop' the boat and maintain position.

METHOD 1   Heaving to ■ 255

In general, back a jib or staysail, and sheet in the mainsail ■ **255. The tiller is lashed to leeward.**

See: Heaving to

METHOD 2   Anchoring

See: Anchoring

METHOD 3   A sea anchor

Stream a sea anchor from either the bow or the stern. **See: Sea anchor**

METHOD 4   Drifting

The boat can be left to drift with the helm lashed alee.

METHOD 5   Sailing with the mainsail ■ 256

The mainsail is sheeted in hard, and the helm lashed alee.

NOTE:

A boat hove to or lying to is still by law underway even if she is making no way.

M

Man overboard!

International Code of Signals

'O'

OSCAR

'MAN OVERBOARD!'

Red

Yellow

■ 257

Emergency action

Do *not* turn immediately.

Throw *some* buoyancy aids over the side.

Also throw any brightly colored objects – such as cockpit cushions, bottles, oilskins, clothing – in the water which will float and mark the spot.

At least one person should keep his eyes *only* on the man in the water.

Start the engine.

Then begin to maneuver.

The basic 'man overboard!' maneuver ■ 258

Immediately, turn upwind ■ 258A.

■ 258 *The basic 'man overboard!' maneuver*

Sail on a circular course which will put you to windward of the man in the water ■ **258B.**

Come about, but leave the jib backed.

When directly to windward of the man in the water, let fly the mainsheet and put the helm to leeward ■ **258C.**

In this 'heave to' position the boat will drift broadside toward the man in the water.

Drift can be corrected by hauling and slackening the mainsheet or using the rudder.

When racing with the spinnaker up, none of these steps can be taken quickly. If an old magazine is at hand, pages thrown into the water every few seconds will create a trail in the water that can be followed backward to the man – even in thick weather.

NOTE:

The man in the water can use the slackened main sheet to help him climb on board.

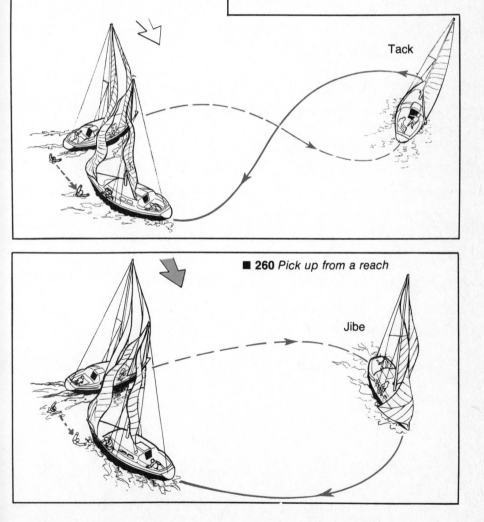

■ 259 *Pick up from a reach*

Tack

■ 260 *Pick up from a reach*

Jibe

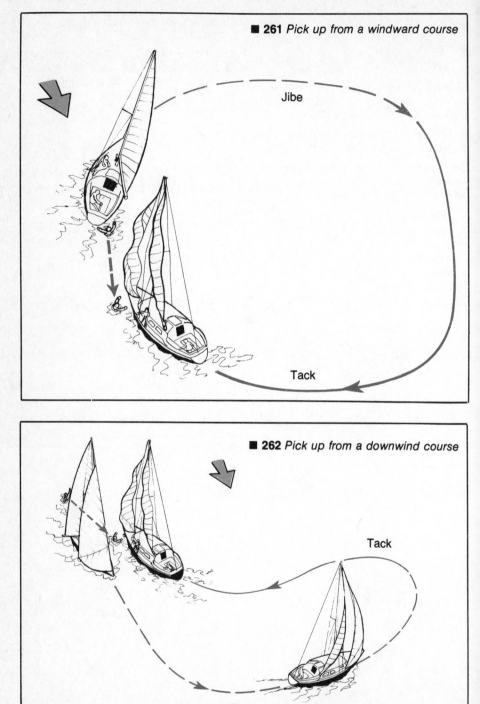

■ **261** *Pick up from a windward course*

Jibe

Tack

■ **262** *Pick up from a downwind course*

Tack

The man overboard is in sight

Pick up from a reach ■ **259, 260.**

Pick up from a windward course ■ **261**

Pick up from a downwind course ■ **262**

The man overboard is not in sight ■ **263, 264, 265**

Fix your position.

Note time and course.

If little wind, no current, and good visibility

Sail, or preferably motor, on a reciprocal course.

If conditions are unfavorable

Begin a planned search pattern at once.

As a general rule, one should sail back well *past* the estimated point at which the man went overboard.

Then the boat should sail back and forth across his estimated course on parallel tracks.

These tracks should be timed, either by a verbal count or a watch.

The first track should be only half that of all of the remaining tracks. The distance between tracks must be carefully calculated to be clearly within the limits of visibility.

Searching from a windward course ■ **263**

■ **263** *Searching from a windward course*

Leeway

Searching from a reach ■ 264

■ **264** *Searching from a reach*

Searching from a downwind course ■ 265

■ **265** *Searching from a downwind course*

NOTE:

Floating safety gear will probably drift faster to leeward than the man in the water. Hence, if life rings, etc., are found first, the survivor is more than likely somewhere to windward.

Life rings should have small drogues attached to reduce their speed downward.

For the man in the water

Remove any weights from pockets.

Remain fully clothed. As a general rule, clothing will keep the skin temperature 4–5 degrees above the water temperature.

Remove any brightly colored garments which can be used for signaling.

Do *not* swim after the boat. Conserve energy, especially if the water is cold. Float on your back with your head into the waves.

Don't shout, as this will also tire you out.

In bad weather or poor visibility, a whistle attached to the crewman's pocket clasp knife may well save his life. A blow on the whistle can guide the yacht back to his position.

For a temporary set of water wings, remove your trousers, knot the legs, then whip them over your head and into the water. Lie in the crotch.

If you receive a line, tie a one-handed bowline. **See: Bowline**

NOTE:

Don't panic. Remember that when in the water one's horizon is very near – in a calm sea, perhaps no more than a mile. The boat may therefore seem to sail out of sight before turning.

Bringing the man on board
■ 266, 267, 268

On small boats pick up the survivor on the *windward* side or the *stern*.

On larger boats, on the *lee* side.

Stop the engine.

Slacken the lifelines.

Don't lower a rope; lower a bight with a

■ **266** *Winching the survivor on board*

■ **267** *Hoisting the survivor on board with a mainsail*

bowline on the end, with both ends securely cleated on deck, or with one end wound onto a cockpit winch ■ **266.**

If the survivor is wearing a safety harness

Attach a halyard to it and haul him on board.

If the survivor is weak or injured

Lower a bosun's chair secured to the topping lift or a halyard.

Lower a jib, genoa, or mainsail – removed from its track – into the water. The jib or genoa should be well sheeted home, and a larger genoa is preferable to a small jib ■ **267, 268**

A half-inflated dinghy can be thrown in the water and used as an aid.

■ **268** *Hoisting the survivor on board with the genoa*

Getting on board by yourself

Do not try to hoist yourself on board, that is, pull yourself up with your arms.

Go to the lee side.

Take hold of the toe rail or a stanchion, then lean back in the water, kick a heel over the rail or behind a stanchion.

Pull yourself on board with your legs.

NOTE:

When making a passage or sailing single-handed, tow a dinghy, or a line of about 100ft. (30 meters) should be towed behind the boat with a loop and/or a float, such as an empty plastic bottle, on the end ■ **269.**

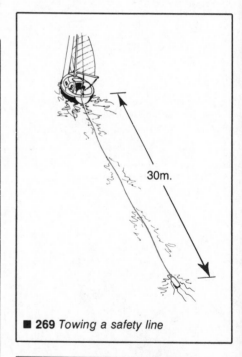

30m.

■ **269** *Towing a safety line*

Mast

See: Climbing the mast, Dismasting, Rigging failure

Medical assistance

International Code of Signals

'W'   ■ 270
WHISKY
'I REQUIRE MEDICAL ASSISTANCE!'

Blue
White
Red

'AN'   ■ 271
ALPHA NOVEMBER
'I NEED A DOCTOR.'

White   Blue

Blue
White

Medical emergencies

See: Antibiotics, Antiseptics, Appendicitis, Artificial respiration, Burns, Constipation, Death, Diarrhea, Ears, Evacuation, Exposure, Eyes, Fatigue, Fishhook injuries, Fractures, Frostbite, Hemorrhages, Heat exhaustion, Immersion foot, Infection, Injections, Medical assistance, Medical kit, Pain killers, Poisoned fish, Scurvy, Seasickness, Shock, Sleeping pills, Sprains, Sterilization, Sunburn, Sunstroke, Toothaches, Tranquilizers, Tropical jellyfish stings, Urine, Vitamins, Water, Wounds

Medical kit

Antibiotics **See: Antibiotics**

Antihistamines **See: Tropical jellyfish stings**

Antiseptics **See: Antiseptics**

Aspirin

Bandages, compresses and waterproof dressings

Burn cream

Burn dressings

Butterfly bandages (very useful)

Constipation tablets **See: Constipation**

Cotton wool

Cough medicine

Diarrhea tablets **See: Diarrhea**

Disposable sterile gloves

Elastic bandages

Epsom salts

Eye drops

Eye ointment

Forceps

Foot powder

Gauze

Indigestion tablets

Milk of magnesia

Needle, suture and catgut

Pain killers **See: Pain killers**

Petroleum gauze

Plaster

Safety pins

Scissors

Seasickness tablets **See: Seasickness**

Splints

Stay-awake tablets **See: Fatigue**

Sticking plasters

Surgical detergent

Suntan oil

Thermometer

Throat lozenges

Tincture of iodine

Tourniquet

Tranquilizers **See: Tranquilizers**

Vitamins

Wound dressings

Morse code

Morse Code

A ● ▬	N ▬ ●	1 ● ▬ ▬ ▬ ▬
B ▬ ● ● ●	O ▬ ▬ ▬	2 ● ● ▬ ▬ ▬
C ▬ ● ▬ ●	P ● ▬ ▬ ●	3 ● ● ● ▬ ▬
D ▬ ● ●	Q ▬ ▬ ● ▬	4 ● ● ● ● ▬
E ●	R ● ▬ ●	5 ● ● ● ● ●
F ● ● ▬ ●	S ● ● ●	6 ▬ ● ● ● ●
G ▬ ▬ ●	T ▬	7 ▬ ▬ ● ● ●
H ● ● ● ●	U ● ● ▬	8 ▬ ▬ ▬ ● ●
I ● ●	V ● ● ● ▬	9 ▬ ▬ ▬ ▬ ●
J ● ▬ ▬ ▬	W ● ▬ ▬	0 ▬ ▬ ▬ ▬ ▬
K ▬ ● ▬	X ▬ ● ● ▬	
L ● ▬ ● ●	Y ▬ ● ▬ ▬	
M ▬ ▬	Z ▬ ▬ ● ●	

Morse code by flags

Separation of dots and/or dashes to mark the end of a letter.

Separation of letters, groups or words.

Erase signal – by the transmitter.
Repeat signal – by the receiver.

Mouth-to-mouth resuscitation

See: Artificial respiration

N

Nautical almanac (or Perpetual Almanac from Appendix of Bowdich)

Out of date

In the back pages of the almanac, following the year's entries, are instructions which permit the data to be used in the following year. An almanac that is out of date by a multiple of four years can be used for sun and stars without correction.

For the sun

Use the figures under the same date, but count *back* 5hrs. 48mins. from the GMT of observation. Then add 87 degrees to the GHA found in the almanac.

For the stars

Using the same date and time, calculate the GHA and declination. Then subtract 15′ 1 from the GHA The declination remains unchanged.

Lost

Sight Reduction Tables HO-249 (AP 3270)

Volume I contains a table from which one can work out the GHA of Aries during the table's period of validity which is five years from date of issue.

Volumes II and III contain tables for the GHA and Declination of the Sun, valid until the year 2000.

Numbers

	DEUTSCH	ENGLISH	FRANÇAIS	NEDERLANDS	DANSK	ITALIANO	ESPAÑOL	PORTUGUÊS
1	eins	one	un	een	en	uno	uno	um
2	zwei	two	deux	twee	to	due	dos	dois
3	drei	three	trois	drie	tre	tre	tres	três
4	vier	four	quatre	vier	fire	quattro	cuatro	quatro
5	fünf	five	cinq	vijf	fem	cinque	cinco	cinco
6	sechs	six	six	zes	seks	sei	seis	seis
7	sieben	seven	sept	zeven	syv	sette	siete	sete
8	acht	eight	huit	acht	otte	otto	ocho	oito
9	neun	nine	neuf	negen	ni	nove	nueve	nove
10	zehn	ten	dix	tien	ti	dieci	diez	dez
11	elf	eleven	onze	elf	elleve	undici	once	onze
12	zwölf	twelve	douze	twaalf	tolv	dodici	doce	doze
13	dreizehn	thirteen	treize	dertien	tretten	tredici	trece	treze
14	vierzehn	fourteen	quatorze	veertien	fjorten	quattordici	catorce	catorze
15	fünfzehn	fifteen	quinze	vijftien	femten	quindici	quince	quinze
16	sechzehn	sixteen	seize	zestien	seksten	sedici	dieciséis	dezaseis
17	siebzehn	seventeen	dix-sept	zeventien	sytten	diciassette	diecisiete	dezasete
18	achtzehn	eighteen	dix-huit	achttien	atten	diciotto	dieciocho	dezoito
19	neunzehn	nineteen	dix-neuf	negentien	nitten	diciannove	diecinueve	dezanove
20	zwanzig	twenty	vingt	twintig	tyve	venti	veinte	vinte
30	dreißig	thirty	trente	dertig	tredive	trenta	treinta	trinta
40	vierzig	forty	quarante	veertig	fyrre	quaranta	cuaranta	quarenta
50	fünfzig	fifty	cinquante	vijftig	halvtreds	cinquanta	cincuenta	cinquenta
60	sechzig	sixty	soixante	zestig	tres	sessanta	sesenta	sessenta
70	siebzig	seventy	soixante-dix	zeventig	halvfjerds	settanta	setenta	setenta
80	achtzig	eighty	quatre-vingt	tachtig	firs	ottanta	ochenta	oitenta
90	neunzig	ninety	quatre-vingt-dix	negentig	halvfems	novanta	noventa	noventa
100	einhundert	one hundred	cent	honderd	hundrede	cento	cient	cem
1000	tausend	thousand	mille	duizend	tusind	mille	mil	mil

O

Oil

Pouring oil onto the sea can be advantageous in certain situations:

Maneuvering alongside another boat in heavy weather.

Hove to in heavy weather.

Passing through a stretch of heavy surf.

Crossing a bar.

Type and amount

The most effective kinds of oil are animal, vegetable or fish oils. Failing those, lubricating oil should be used.

As a rough guide, 1 quart or 1 liter of heavy oil will cover approximately 24 square yards (20 square meters), that is, about the deck space of two yachts. In a bad sea releasing small amounts of oil may not offer much relief.

Principle

A heavy, low-viscosity oil will float on the surface of the sea and spread out into a thin film with a high tensile strength. This produces an often extraordinary calming effect – but *only* on the tendency of waves to crest and break. It will *not* in any way reduce their size.

NOTE:

Often the problem with releasing oil is that the boat and the oil slick may drift at different rates. To be effective the slick must extend windward. It will not help much in surf or on a bar with an onshore wind unless you are entering under a deal of power, nor with an offshore wind unless you are leaving the land under power.

Oil bags ■ 272, 273, 274, 275, 276

Fill a plastic container $\frac{1}{2}$ to $\frac{3}{4}$ full of heavy oil.

Wrap it in several layers of old rags ■ **272.**

Sew it into a canvas bag.

Just before using, puncture the container several times with a marlin spike ■ **273.**

Preparing an oil bag

■ 272

■ 273

■ **274** *Streaming oil bags when lying ahull*   ■ **275** *Streaming oil bags when running and towing warps*   ■ **276** *Streaming oil bags when lying-to a sea anchor*

If lying ahull

Stream the bags to windward ■ **274.**

If running and towing warps

Stream the bags from the bow ■ **275.**

If lying to a sea anchor

Stream the bags from the sea anchor ■ **276.**

Oil hose ■ 277

Fill a length of old plastic hose, 1½–2in. (4–5cm.) in diameter with oil and seal both ends.

Tie a buoyancy aid – plastic bottle, fender, lifejacket or life ring – to the outer end.

Puncture the hose as it is streamed over the side.

Tow it at least 33ft. (10 meters) behind the boat.

Pumping out oil

Oil can be pumped out of a windward seacock, such as a toilet or sink drain, or simply poured into the bilge and discharged by a bilge pump.

For swimming in an oily sea **See: Abandon ship!**

■ **277** *Streaming an oil hose*

P

Pain killers

Pain killers are known as analgesics, drugs that relieve pain without loss of consciousness. Narcotics depress the brain cells involved in pain perception and somewhat affect a person's sensations of pain. Synthetic narcotics usually promote relaxation; may cause constipation.

NOTE:

Do *not* use narcotics for head injuries. Narcotics are respiratory depressants.

DOSAGE
Moderate

England
Aspirin | 600mg. or 2 tablets 4 times/day

Distalgesic | 1 tablet 4 times/day

Paracetamol | 2 tablets every 4 hours

Strong

Codeine | 30–60mg. 3 times/day

Moderate

France
Aspirine | 500mg. or 2 tablets 4 times/day

Diantalvic | 1 tablet 4 times/day

Dolipren | 2 tablets every 4 hours

DOSAGE
Strong

Codeine | 30–60mg. 3 times/day

Moderate

Germany
Aspirin | 600mg. 2 tablets 4 times/day

Novalgin | 1 tablet 4 times/day

Ben-u-ron | 1–2 tablets 2–3 times/day

Strong

Eukodal | ½ tablet once/day

Moderate

U.S.
Aspirin | 600mg. or 2 tablets 4–6 times/day

Acetamino-phen | 600mg. or 2 tablets 4 times/day

Strong

Codeine | 30–60mg. 3 times/day

NOTE:

Aspirin can be surprisingly effective when used in conjunction with codeine. *Dosage:* 600mg. aspirin and 30mg. codeine every four hours.

Pilot

International code of signals

‘G’
GOLF
‘I REQUIRE A PILOT.’

‘H’
HOTEL
‘I HAVE A PILOT ON BOARD.’

Yellow   Blue

For light patterns of pilot vessels **See: Lights**

■ 278

Pilot vessel on duty

Pilot vessel making way
2 minutes   2 minutes

Pilot vessel stopped but not at anchor
2 minutes   2 minutes

Pilot vessel at anchor

1 minute
4 short blasts
5 seconds

1 minute
4 short blasts
5 seconds

Poisoned fish

See also: Fish

Unfortunately, in tropical waters nearly any fish worth eating – mullet, eel, herring, shark, turtle, shellfish, etc. – *can* be poisoned, and there appears to be no way of knowing beforehand whether or not a fish is contaminated.

One thing is clear: the phenomenon is regional, to such an extent that fish on one side of a lagoon or bay can be poisoned and on the other side be completely healthy. Before fishing in coastal waters or lagoons it is often wise to seek local advice.

When in doubt

Do not eat the viscera – heart, liver, etc.

Eat smaller varieties of fish, those of less than 2lb. (1kg.)

Soak the cleaned, filleted fish in fresh water for at least an hour, changing the water several times.

If poisoned

Immediately induce vomiting by:

Sticking a finger down your throat.

or

Drinking a solution of two teaspoons salt in a glass of water.

Take three tablespoons of olive oil to induce diarrhea.

Then seek local aid for an antidote.

Pole star

See: Stars

Propellers

If a line becomes wound around the propeller ■ 279, 280

First, bring end on deck. Put the engine in neutral, turn it over by hand, and try to unwind the line by pulling on it.

If it must be cut

For coils of wire or cable *only* a hacksaw and new blade will be effective.

For tightly wound and compressed ropes a hacksaw is best, but an old knife with a chipped blade or a bread knife will also be effective.

Procedure

If the boat is of light displacement, shifting weight to the bow, such as that of the crew, can raise the propeller closer to the surface where it will be easier to work on ■ 279.

■ **279** *Shifting weight to raise the stern*

An inflatable dinghy, half inflated and capsized, can make an excellent working platform ■ **280**.

A face mask and/or snorkel can make the task easier.

Tools should be secured with lines so that both hands can be free to fend off the boat.

WARNING:

When working over the side, wear a safety harness.

Also, for protection against barnacle scrapes, a shirt, gloves and woolen hat.

A kapok or cork lifejacket tied around your head will offer some protection against a bouncing stern.

Pumps

The engine's water pump as a bilge pump ■ 281, 282

Close the water intake seacock.

Remove the hose and place it in the bilge. An extra length of hose may need to be added.

Prepare an intake screen in advance and keep it with the emergency gear.

If possible, place a piece of screen or fine

■ **280**

net over the end as these pumps are susceptible to clogging.

Start the engine.

WARNING:

Engine cooling pumps are not high-capacity pumps. Engines of 10–50 h.p. normally deliver only 5–23 gallons (20–90 liters) per minute, less than that of a manual bilge pump. However, since it can be an extra hand, a permanent system with a switch can easily be installed ■ **282**.

For the capacities of different kinds of pumps **See: Holes**

■ **281** *Using the engine cooling pump as an emergency bilge pump*

■ **282**

R

Radar reflectors

Mounting

The best location is at the masthead.

Failing that, the reflector should be secured:
In a stable position.
As high as possible.
Where it will not be blanketed by metal spars or wet sails.

An octahedral reflector should *not* be mounted in a point-up attitude, rather its base remains in a flat box-like or 'catch-rain' position ■ **283.**

The surfaces must be kept clean and free from corrosion and strictly at 90 degrees to each other.

NOTE:

The smallest commercial reflector properly mounted 14ft. (4 meters) above the deck will return a strong echo to a ship five miles away. At a pinch, an aluminized plastic 'space blanket' will give a reflection.

WARNING:

1 – Bits or strips of aluminum foil, biscuit tins, jerry cans, or other metallic garbage hoisted aloft can be considered worthless. Also metal spars and masts are not substitutes, as a mast would only return a signal if the boat were not heeled.

2 – In conditions of bad weather and visibility you are less likely to be detected at extremely close range than farther out. Also rain and snow tend to reduce the reflector's effectiveness.

Principle

A radar reflector is nothing more than a set of metal mirrors, aligned at 90-degree angles, so that a beam striking one of them is reflected on the next until it is finally returned to the source along the same path as it came. For this reason, it is absolutely essential that the plates be positioned at perfect right angles. An error of a few degrees can reduce the effectiveness of a reflector by as much as half.

The larger the reflector, the more beams returned. Since effectiveness increases with area, a reflector 20in. (50cm.) a side is almost three times more effective than a 12in. (30cm.) one.

■ **283** *A radar reflector mounted in the correct 'catch rain' position*

Radio direction finder

Homing

Place the ferrite aerial of the unit parallel with the fore and aft line of the boat. Swing the boat until the unit registers a 'null' – the point of weakest reception. Read the course from the boat's compass.

WARNING:

1 – Bearings taken an hour before to an hour after sunrise or sunset should be regarded as suspect due to 'Night Effect' – a tendency of the ionosphere to change its properties at those times.

2 – Steel or aluminum boats may have unpredictable errors. These can be minimized by always taking bearing from the same location on board.

3 – If the bearing of a radio beacon makes an acute angle with the coast, it may be slightly deflected. The error – usually not more than 5 degrees – will be in the direction of the coast.

NOTE:

When three or more bearings result in a 'cocked hat', your position is more than likely:

A – Within the triangle ■ **284.**

B – Closer to the shorter sides – 'the shorter, the closer' ■ **285.**

C – Closer to the bearing with the smallest distance to range ratio, that is, the bearing which has the smallest result when the approximate distance to beacon is divided by the beacon range.

■ 284

■ 285

■ 286

■ **287** *A makeshift antenna for a radio direction finder*

A makeshift antenna ■ 287

Rainwater

Collecting rainwater at sea

Materials

83ft. (25 meters) of insulated wire

Four large screws

Procedure

On an athwartship bulkhead, place the screws in a square about 24in. (60cm.) on a side.

Begin at the bottom and wind the wire around the square about 10 times, ending in the same position you began.

Attach the two leads to the receiver's loop connection.

Tune in a strong station, then *swing the boat* to find the null point, that is, the point of weakest reception.

The bearing to the station can be read from the boat's compass.

METHOD 1

Hang a bucket near the gooseneck, but wait a few minutes for the salt to wash off the mainsail. Raising the topping lift can greatly increase the flow ■ **288.**

■ **288**

METHOD 2

Tie a pre-prepared plastic sheet between the shrouds, but leave enough extra line at the corners so that it can be adjusted to face the wind ■ **289.**

■ 289

METHOD 3

Lash two spars or oars together and fasten the plastic sheet between them ■ **290.**

■ 290

Collecting rainwater at anchor

METHOD 1

Construct a rain-collecting sheet from plastic or the sun awning with a hole in the center which is joined to a piece of plastic hose. Tie the sheet between the shrouds and run the tubing into the tank or a jerry can ■ **291.**

■ 291

METHOD 2

Construct gutters for the coach roof by cutting several feet (or a few meters) of plastic tubing lengthwise ■ **292.**

■ 292

METHOD 3

Cover the cockpit with a sail, fastened to the coach roof and lifelines and allow it to drain into a bucket on the floor of the cockpit ■ **293.**

NOTE:

In emergencies, dry clothes or towels can be laid on the deck, then wrung into a bucket later.

■ **293**

Reefing and sail reduction

See also: Heavy weather

The moment to reduce sail

If going to windward or reaching, when

The boat is heeling over too far.
The boat is moving too fast for the seas.
The sails are too light for the wind.
The motion of the boat has become uncomfortable.

If the boat is running it is easy to have a false sense of security and a false estimation of wind and sea speed.

As a general rule, never carry more sail while running than would be carried while beating or reaching.

Principle

Wind force – thrust – increases 2–3 times faster than speed. Thus, reduction in sail does not necessarily mean a reduction in speed.

Procedure

As the weather becomes worse, low-cut headsails should be replaced by high-cut ones to prevent possible damage from the sea or wind.

The center of effort, that is, the sail area center, should be lowered and moved forward amidships.

For the safety of the main mast, some sail should be left on to prevent whipping in high seas.

Revolving storms

See: Law of storms

Rigging failures

Emergency action

Should any part of the standing rigging – shrouds, forestays, backstays, the spreaders, a turnbuckle, or the cable – part or show signs of parting:

If the seas are calm

Take down all sail at once. Leave headsails up if headstay or forestay lets go.

If the seas are rough

It is better to continue sailing than to risk the strain which might be put on the mast by rolling and pitching in the waves, even with a sea anchor streamed from the bow or stern.

If a shroud has parted

More than likely it will be the weather one.

Go immediately to the other tack, and bring the wind abeam. At that point the rigging will again be at near normal strength.

WARNING:

Jibing can be dangerous, especially with a flexible mast. Generally, the few seconds gained are not worth the risk.

If a forestay has parted

Turn downwind so that the strain of the mast is placed on the backstay. Attach the shackle of a spare halyard to the stem head fitting, and take the strain on it.

If a backstay has parted

Bring the boat up into the wind.

Drop the headsails.

If the boat has running backstays, set up the leeward one as well.

If a turnbuckle has given way

Attach a shackle to the chainplate in place of the turnbuckle jaw, and pass a length of rigging wire through the shackle.

Form the other end into a bight with wire rope clips and connect it to the existing wire by means of:

1 – A block and tackle. **See: Block and tackle**

2 – A lanyard. **See: Lanyard**

3 – Another turnbuckle ■ **294.**

4 – A lashing ■ **295.**

If a splice has given way

Bend the broken end of the wire to form an eye which can be either spliced or held in place with wire rope clips. **See: Wire rope clips**

If the turnbuckle will open

Open it, and connect it to the new eye in the cable by means of:

1 – Another turnbuckle ■ **296.**

2 – A chain of shackles ■ **297.**

3 – A length of chain with a shackle on each end ■ **298.**

4 – A lashing.

Take up the slack with the turnbuckle.

If the turnbuckle will not open

Attach one end of a strong piece of cord to the eye of the wire and the other to a shackle fixed to the turnbuckle.

Take many turns of line.

Insert a marlin spike or screwdriver between the strands and rotate it like a Spanish windlass to take up the slack ■ **299.** Use wrenches or screwdrivers to prevent the turnbuckle and eye from twisting.

When the wire is taut, join the eye to the shackle with a chain of shackles, lashing or lanyard.

See: Lanyard

If one or more strands of wire has broken

Lay another piece of wire alongside it, stretch it as tightly as possible, then clamp it in place with wire rope clips. **See: Bulldog clamps (wire rope clips)**

Tape the loose ends to protect the sails ■ **300.**

■ 294

■ 295

■ 296

■ 297

■ 298

■ 299

■ 300

- 301
- 302
- 303
- 304

If a cable has broken

Bend both ends of the cable into eyes and fasten them with wire rope clips. **See: Bulldog clamps (wire rope clips)**

Join the two eyes together with:
A turnbuckle ■ **301.**
A strong lashing ■ **302.**
A short length of chain ■ **303.**
A chain of shackles ■ **304.**

Take up the slack with the turnbuckle.

Cutting wire rope or cable ■ 305

With wire cutters

Make a whipping $1\frac{1}{4}$in. (3cm.) on either side of the cutting point. Whip away from the cutting point. Then use the wire cutters.

With a cold chisel

Make a whipping $1\frac{1}{4}$in. (3cm.) on either side of the cutting point.

Place the wire on a hard surface such as a steel blade, anchor winch, big hammer or deck fitting.

Strike the wire a few times to flatten it.

Hold the chisel on the surface and slowly cut the strands.

■ 305 *Cutting wire rope or cable*

NOTE:

Many expensive wire cutters cannot cut stainless-steel 1×19 rigging, but a cold chisel will always do the job.

Temporary repair of a shroud or headstay

METHOD 1 ■ 306

Shackle a free foresail halyard to the chain plate or the headstay fitting. If there is no place to attach the shackle, the connection must be made with a lashing.

Take up the slack on the halyard winch until the line is taut. Although the halyard will probably bear an enormous amount of strain, it is still no replacement for the stay and therefore should not be set up too tightly.

METHOD 2 ■ 307

Shackle a free halyard to the headstay's fitting, and tie a length of line to the other end.

Attach a block to the headstay fitting and run the line through the block, then onto the halyard winch.

METHOD 3 ■ 308

If the halyards are in the mast, or unavailable, and the break is at a reachable height, then quick repair can be made with a small block and tackle and wire rope clips.

Make an eye in the long end of the shroud or headstay with wire rope clips. **See: Bulldog clamps (wire rope clips)** or

Tie one end of the block and tackle to the cable with a rolling hitch **(See: Knots)** 6–8in. (15–20cm.) above the break. Below that, fasten wire rope clips to the cable to prevent the knot from sliding.

The other end of the block and tackle can be secured to a fitting.

NOTE:

This method saves the use of a halyard.

■ **306** *Replacing a broken headstay with a halyard*

■ **307** *Replacing a broken headstay with a halyard*

■ **308** *Replacing a broken shroud or stay with a block and tackle*

Temporary repair of the backstay ■ 309

METHOD 1

Shackle the topping lift to the backstay fitting.

Attach some line to the other end, and take up the slack on the halyard winch.

METHOD 2 ■ 310

If the boat has a long boom, the mast can be securely supported by leaving the topping lift shackled to the boom.

Tie the free end of the topping lift to the outhaul fitting on the end of the boom. It may be necessary to add a length of line.

Draw up the slack and support the mast with the mainsheet.

NOTE:

On modern boats with short booms, the mast may be given additional support by shackling a foresail or spinnaker halyard to the backstay fitting. This will probably involve twisting or bending the masthead block into place, as well as chafing the line, but this may be necessary to prevent further damage.

METHOD 3 ■ 311

If the boat is without a topping lift and a halyard winch as well, the foresail halyard is cleated home to the mast. A bit of extra line is attached to the other end which is taken aft, run through a block, on the backstay fitting and then onto a cockpit winch.

■ **309** *Replacing a broken backstay with the topping lift*

■ **310** *Replacing a broken backstay with the topping lift and winch*

■ **311**

Right of way

See: Collision

Running

Purpose

When sea and wind conditions no longer permit the boat to remain hove to, the decision must be made to run with the storm.

The boat then rides with the wind and seas, and the relative wind and wave speeds are reduced. However, unless the waves are extremely short, the boat will never move at the same speed as the waves. Being pooped and broaching will always be a danger.

Way is kept on, which allows the boat to be steered and to compensate for dangerous cross-seas. How much way – that is, the speed of the boat to be maintained – is a highly debatable subject which is dependent upon the special characteristics of the storm, waves and boat. In general, the shorter the waves, the slower the boat's speed should be. When in doubt, err on the side of slowing down.

The three basic tactics for running

Running under reduced sail.

Running under bare poles.

Running while streaming warps.

WARNING:

When running, the weakest parts of the boat – stern, cockpit and after cabin bulkhead – are presented to the seas. Never leave the companionway open, and always keep the cockpit drains clear.

Running under reduced sail

Take the seas dead astern or slightly on the quarter which will lead you away from the storm center.

The boat should not carry more sail when running than when beating into the storm.

Usually, the guide for when to reduce sail further is the size of the seas rather than the strength of the wind.

The last sail to come off is the staysail or jib sheeted flat to the mast. **See: Reefing and sail reduction**

Running under bare poles

All sail is taken down, the mainsail stripped from the boom, and the sail bags stowed below.

The boat is steered, and thus takes each wave as it comes.

Even stripped of all sails, the boat will still have considerable windage due to her freeboard, mast and rigging, and hence can make considerable speed. If the speed is too great, warps may have to be streamed.

Running while streaming

warps ■ 312

This will greatly reduce the forward movement of the boat. The distinction between streaming warps and streaming a sea anchor is that the former breaks or retards the boat's speed, while the latter tends to stop her.

Streaming warps will help the boat keep her stern into the wind and also have a quieting effect on the seas astern.

WARNING:

If the warps cause an excessive strain they may rob the boat of some of her buoyancy. **See: Sea anchor**

Procedure

The warps may be streamed from either quarter, tied in a bight, or fastened to a

■ **312** *Running while streaming warps*

bridle. They should be well secured to deck fittings or cockpit winches as the strain can be enormous.

The warps should be as thick as possible.

Knots can be tied to increase the drag.

The length will have to be adjusted to the sea and wind conditions. Normally, between 250 and 800ft. (80 and 250 meters) of warp is required.

More than one warp can be streamed.

Single warps with such items as life rings, fenders, tires, or sailbags tied to the ends can also be used.

More than likely the boat will still need to be steered.

Rules of the road

See: Collision

Safety harness

Points

Points to clip onto

Jackstays (see next page)

Shrouds

Lifelines

Pin rail

Points which can be dangerous to clip onto (as they can trip the snap hook open)

Stanchion bases with welded legs

Chainplates

Pulpit

Stern pulpits

Eye bolts

Deck fittings

Points *not* to clip onto

Deck cleats

Mast cleats

Wooden handrails

Turnbuckles

NOTE:

Looping the safety line around the fitting and clipping the hook onto the line will greatly reduce the strength of the line ■ **313.**

■ 313

■ **314** *Points for safety harness clip-on*

■ **315** *Rigging a temporary jackstay*

■ **316** *Rigging a temporary jackstay*

A temporary jackstay ■ 315, 316

Use strong rope or wire cable.

Run a line lengthwise on each side of the boat, shackling it securely to deck fittings.

If necessary, a single or double line will serve – from the bow, to the mast, over the coach roof, then to the cockpit.

Always clip on *before* leaving the cockpit foredeck to the cleat on the fantail, so the safety harness clip is unobstructed as a man moves fore and aft.

Leave the mainsheet slack, and back the jib. In small boats it is preferable to back the mainsail instead ■ **317.**

Point the rudder in the *opposite direction* to that in which you wish the bow to turn.

Sail reduction

See: Reefing

Sailing backward

For downwind berthing stern to, or coming out of irons

A quick and simple way is to rig a dockline from the mooring cleat on the

Sail repair

Tears and rips ■ **319**

Materials

Thread.

Needles.

Beeswax.

Sewing palm.

Procedure

Double, even quadruple, the thread.

Wax the thread by drawing it several times across the beeswax.

Make a knot in the end and sew using a sailmaker's darn (herringbone stitch).

Make 5–6 stitches per inch (2.5cm.).

■ **319** *A sailmaker's darn – herringbone stitch*

Any tear longer than 2in. (5cm.) which is not along a seam should be patched.

■ **317** *Sailing backward*

Patching ■ 320, 321, 322

Materials

Thread.

Needles.

Beeswax.

Sewing palm.

Patch: this should be approximately the same weight cloth as the sail being repaired. It should be large enough to extend 2in. (5cm.) on either side of the tear.

Procedure

If possible, sew the break closed with a blanket stitch ■ 320.

If the patch is cut from a synthetic fabric, hot-seal the edges with an iron, soldering iron, or screwdriver heated on the stove. Failing that, turn the edges under.

If the patch is cut from canvas, miter the corners, then turn the edges under.

If corners of a rectangular patch are cut off at a 45-degree angle before turning under, a neat seam is formed and the corners of the patch lie flat.

Place the patch on the sail with its warp and woof lined up with that of the sail.

Hold the patch in place by means of tape, pins, or stitches in the corners ■ 321.

Sew the patch on with an overhand or seam stitch ■ 322.

WARNING:

Even though Dacron sails are harder and will take more punishment than canvas, the seams of synthetic fabrics are highly vulnerable. Whereas stitches in cotton or flax tend to sink in and become a part of the cloth, stitches in Dacron stand out, and if too large a thread is used, make little holes of their own. For this reason, three rows of stitches on a seam are required. The two outer ones are meant to protect the inner one.

Patching a sail

■ 320

■ 321

■ 322

■ 323 *Patching a tear along the bolt rope*

For tears along the bolt rope

■ 323

Wrap the patch around the bolt rope, then sew it through from both sides and along the edge of the rope.

For tears along the headboard

■ 324

Fold a large patch over the headboard which covers the tear on both sides. Stitch along the base of the headboard, fold in the flaps of the patch, then sew through the headboard holes.

■ 324 *Patching a tear along the headboard*

For tears along a batten pocket

■ 325

Remove the stitches along the edge of the pocket and slide in the patch. Sew the patch on, then resew the pocket in place.

■ 325 *Patching a tear along a batten pocket*

For tears at the tack or clew

METHOD 1

Sew in a round thimble, install the liner, then flare out the edges ■ 326.

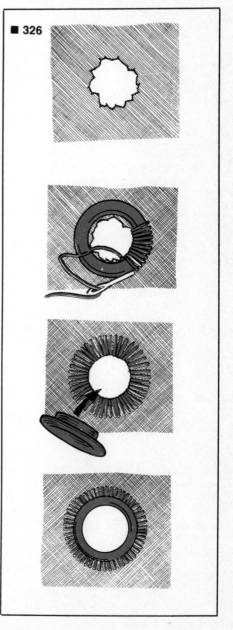

■ 326

METHOD 2

Sew a piece of rope around the hole ■ **327** either around the rope or, if possible, through it.

METHOD 4

Sew a shackle which will serve as a sheet point either over the hole or to the bolt rope ■ **329.**

METHOD 3

Make a rope cringle around the bolt rope. This can be fabricated as shown from a length of (■ **328**) strong line.

NOTE:

To reduce stress, pass the sheet several times through the clew, then secure it with a bowline.

METHOD 5

Fold the clew several times, bunch the sail together and lash it securely ■ **330.**

Long tears, blown-out sails and weakened sailcloth

Materials

A strong, water-resistant contact glue.

Patching material. If not enough is available, a sailbag makes a good substitute.

'Spinnaker tape,' which comes with adhesive already applied, is quick, very strong and holds surprisingly well. It can be sewn in place for more permanence.

Procedure

Clean the gluing surfaces with fresh water and let them dry.

If the break is along a seam, don't use a patch.

Spread the glue evenly on both surfaces and let it nearly dry.

■ 330

Press the two surfaces together.

To make a solid bond, pound the entire joint with a block of wood and a hammer.

For easy sewing

Lay the sail and patch over a cutting board across your knees, and place the seam along the edge.

■ 331 *Holding the sail taut with a shock cord and hook*

Hold the sail taut by means of a shock cord and hook ■ 331.

For fast sewing on heavy cloth

Hold the sail vertically, and with a man on either side, each armed with a sewing palm and a pair of pliers, push and pull the needles back and forth.

Chafe

On the seams

Cover both sides of the seam with sail tape (nylon or Dacron) or spinnaker tape and stitch it lightly in place.

On sails

Once a chafe mark appears, cover the area on *both* sides with a patch of light Dacron.

Prevention

Rig a boom vang so that the sail will lose its tendency to ride up and down on the shrouds and spreaders.

Cover spreader ends with tape, a leather bag or tennis balls.

Cover turnbuckles with tape, plastic hose, or rags.

See: Baggywrinkle, chafe

Salvage

Misconceptions

The acceptance of a towline from another boat does not *automatically* entitle them to claim salvage.

The acceptance of aid from a crew member of another boat does not *automatically* entitle him to claim salvage.

A salvor does not *automatically* become the owner of the property he rescues.

Principle

By law and custom sailors are bound to do everything in their power to help save lives at sea, but they are not obligated to save property.

There is no legal parallel ashore.

For example, should a man in a volunteer fire brigade help put out a fire in your house, he will have no legal claim on your property. However, if he puts out a fire on your boat which is afloat in the harbor he could well be entitled to a salvage award.

To make a valid claim a salvor must show:

The ship was in peril.

His decision to come to the aid – of the property – was voluntary.

He risked his own life and/or property to save the ship.

His efforts were successful.

The degree of the ship's peril, the extent of the salvor's risk, his time, effort, ultimate success, plus the value of the property saved are important factors which a court will use to determine the amount of a salvage award.

Crew members and passengers of a ship generally do not receive salvage awards for saving their vessel.

Salvage agreements

If the captain of a ship in peril comes to an agreement with a salvor beforehand, that person will have no further salvage rights. A legal contract – such as an agreement for a tow made in the presence of witnesses – takes precedence over a salvage claim.

Often this contract is in the form of the *Lloyd's Open Agreement* which is based on a 'no cure – no pay' arrangement which leaves the amount of the award to be settled later by arbitration. The Lloyd's agreement need not be signed. A verbal accord, such as that hailed between two ships in front of witnesses, is sufficient and binding.

Sculling

If it is not possible to scull with the rudder by wagging the tiller rapidly from side to side, when necessary even a boat of 33ft. (10 meters) or more can be sculled short distances in calm waters with an oar.

The oar must be securely lashed or fitted in a rowlock or notch in the transom.

It need not be on the center line of the boat. For example, on double-enders the oar can be lashed to a stern quarter.

Simply 'sculling' with the tiller (pushing it back and forth) will move quite large boats in calm water. It is no good with a wheel.

Technique ■ 332

Stand facing aft.

Hold the shaft of the oar with both hands.

The blade should be at an angle of about 30 degrees to the transom.

Push the oar to one side so that the blade digs into the water.

Twist your wrist to turn the blade back to an angle of 30 degrees.

Then repeat the process – push and twist, push and twist.

LLOYD'S

NOTES.

1. Insert name of person signing on behalf of owners of property to be salved. The Master should sign wherever possible.

2. The Contractor's name should always be inserted in line 3 and whenever the Agreement is signed by the Master of the Salving vessel or other person on behalf of the Contractor the name of the Master or other person must also be inserted in line 3 before the words " for and on behalf of ". The words " for and on behalf of " should be deleted where a Contractor signs personally.

STANDARD FORM OF

SALVAGE AGREEMENT

(APPROVED AND PUBLISHED BY THE COMMITTEE OF LLOYD'S)

NO CURE—NO PAY

On board the
Dated   19

† See Note 1
above

IT IS HEREBY AGREED between Captain†   for and on
behalf of the Owners of the "   " her cargo and
freight and   for and on behalf of

* See Note 2
above

(hereinafter called " the Contractor " *): —

1. The Contractor agrees to use his best endeavours to salve the
and / or her cargo and take them into   or other
place to be hereafter agreed. The services shall be rendered and accepted as
salvage services upon the principle of " no cure—no pay ". In case of arbitration being
claimed the Contractor's remuneration in the event of success shall be fixed by
arbitration in London in the manner hereinafter prescribed: and any difference
arising out of this Agreement or the operations thereunder shall be referred to
arbitration in the same way. In the event of the services referred to in this Agreement
or any part of such services having been already rendered at the date of this
Agreement by the Contractor to the said vessel and / or her cargo it is agreed that the
provisions of this Agreement shall apply to such services.

2. The Contractor may make reasonable use of the vessel's gear anchors chains
and other appurtenances during and for the purpose of the operations free of expense
but shall not unnecessarily damage abandon or sacrifice the same or any other of the
property the subject of this Agreement.

3. The Master or other person signing this Agreement on behalf of the property
to be salved is not authorised to make or give and the Contractor shall not demand
or take any payment draft or order for or on account of the remuneration.

PROVISIONS AS TO SECURITY

4. The Contractor shall immediately after the termination of the services or
sooner notify the Committee of Lloyd's of the amount for which he requires security
(inclusive of costs, expenses and interest) to be given. Unless otherwise agreed by the
parties such security shall be given to the Committee of Lloyd's, and security so given
shall be in a form approved by the Committee and shall be given by persons firms or
corporations resident in the United Kingdom either satisfactory to the Committee of
Lloyd's or agreed by the Contractor. The Committee of Lloyd's shall not be responsible
for the sufficiency (whether in amount or otherwise) of any security which shall be
given nor for the default or insolvency of any person firm or corporation giving the
same.

5. Pending the completion of the security as aforesaid, the Contractor shall have
a maritime lien on the property salved for his remuneration. The salved property shall

■ **332** *Sculling – push and twist*

Scurvy

Symptoms

Listlessness, fatigue, and a lack of endurance.

Shortness of breath.

Aches and pains in the joints or muscles, particularly at night.

In later stages:
Gums begin to bleed.
Hemorrhages occur in the muscles and joints.
Scars break open.

Wounds refuse to heal.

Medication

Vitamin C – a minimum of 100mg. daily.

NOTE:

Although limes are the traditional preventative on long passages, lemons have substantially more antiscorbutic value. At sea, an intake of 75mg. of vitamin C daily is sufficient to prevent the disease.

Scuttling

If aground in surf, swells or heavy weather and in danger of being broken up, as a last resort the boat must be flooded ■ **333.**

Set the best anchors seaward. **See: Anchoring**

Run lines ashore to hold the boat in position as securely as possible, so that she will neither be driven farther ashore, nor be carried out to sea.

Use floorboards, doors, tabletops, spars or driftwood as wedges to protect the hull as much as possible.

Open all seacocks, portholes and hatchways.

Abandon ship.

As the tide recedes or the weather turns fair, water will drain from the open seacocks and there should be a chance to refloat the boat on the next calm, high tide.

NOTE:
Before abandoning ship, strip the boat of all valuable gear.

Sea anchors

In heavy weather

A sea anchor should be used *only as a last resort* to prevent a boat from making leeway.

Sea anchors produce a tremendous strain on the hull and rigging, and in effect, rob the boat of some of its buoyancy.

When the sea anchor is streamed from the stern, the boat is in danger of being pooped or pitchpoled.

When the sea anchor is streamed from the bow, the boat can easily be thrown backwards and the rudder damaged.

Generally, it is easier to stream and control a sea anchor from the stern. However, boats with narrow hulls, no

■ **333** *Scuttling a boat driven aground*

■ **334** *Matching the length of a sea anchor warp with wavelength*

self-draining cockpit and little buoyancy aft should stream a sea anchor from the bow.

Procedure

The warp

As a general rule, the diameter and material of the sea anchor warp should be the same as that of an anchor warp.

The preferable material is nylon because of its elasticity.

If the seas are 'regular', that is, distances between crests are nearly uniform, the length of the warp should be about one wavelength, or some multiple thereof ■ **334.**

The warp is tied to a strong point on either the bow or stern. See: Towing

WARNING:

The warp must be well protected against chafe. **See: Chafe**

Sails ■ 334

Traditional long keel boats will probably lie well under bare poles while streaming a sea anchor.

Modern yachts have a tendency to sheer off. This can be corrected by either:

■ **335** *Protecting the rudder against a stern sea*

A jib hanked on the backstay and sheeted amidships.

or

A normal jib sheeted amidships.

Rudder ■ 335

If the sea anchor is streamed from the bow, the rudder becomes vulnerable to the seas. The tiller should be lashed amidships with shock cords or rubber straps, so that if the boat is thrown backwards there is some elasticity in the system.

Makeshift sea anchor

A makeshift sea anchor

1 – An old car tire, with or without a weight ■ **336.**

2 – A sail with or without a spar and weight at its head ■ **337.**

3 – Two oars lashed together and weighted ■ **338.**

4 – A plank securely lashed to a small anchor and, if necessary, given some flotation from a lifejacket or a life ring ■ **339.**

5 – Simply lowering the anchor in water far too deep for it to reach bottom has been recommended.

Seacocks

To free a frozen or jammed valve

METHOD 1

Tap it gently with a hammer.

METHOD 2

Consider taking it apart, working fast to lubricate and reassemble, and then pumping the bilge.

METHOD 3

Heat it with a blowtorch, while protecting the surrounding area with wet rags ■ **340.**

METHOD 4

Exert more leverage by lashing a screwdriver, turnbuckle, or piece of pipe or wood to the ring. Be careful not to apply too much pressure and damage the fitting ■ **341.**

A leaky seacock

Unscrew the fitting *only* a few turns.

Wrap the threads with oakum, tape, or if necessary, glue or epoxy.

Tighten the fitting.

■ **341** *Freeing a frozen seacock*

■ **342** *Changing a seacock while the boat is still in the water*

To change a seacock while the boat is in the water ■ 342

METHOD 1

See: Aground, Careening

METHOD 2

Working under water

Tie a rope under the keel, which can be used as a handhold while working under water.

Cut a piece of soft wood in the shape of a conical plug so that the small end just fits into the hull. Small pieces of softwood should be carried aboard routinely.

Knock the plug into the fitting from the outside.

Remove and replace the seacock from inside the hull.

NOTE:

To fit a new plastic hose on a seacock

Place the end in a pot of hot water for a few moments. When it is soft, *immediately* thrust it over the fitting. Secure it with a hose clamp.

To repair a leaky hose ■ 343

Use tape.

or

Cut the hose in two, and trim away any worn material. Join the two ends together by placing a piece of smaller hose or pipe inside them. Clamp both ends with wire or hose clamps.

■ **343** *Repairing a broken or leaky hose*

Seasickness

Symptoms

Headache.

A cold sweat.

A feeling of weakness and apathy.

Nausea and vomiting.

In extreme cases, depression to the point of suicide.

Many victims seem comfortable stationary on deck or flat in their bunks, but nowhere in between.

Treatment

Don't go below. Stay in the fresh air.

Keep warm and dry.

Avoid the sun.

Drink very little.

No alcohol.

Eat small amounts of soft food every few hours.

Close your eyes, or focus only on the horizon.

Medication

NOTE:

Most antiseasickness drugs have proved effective, but since vomiting is nearly always a problem, those in suppository form are often the most useful.

Tranquilizers appear to have little effect in combating seasickness.

	Dosage
England Dramamine	50mg. 1–2 hrs. before departure, then 3 times/day
France Primperan	1 tablet 3 times/day

Dosage

Germany

Bonamine   25mg.=1 tablet
1–2 tablets 1–2 hrs.
before departure, then 3
times/day

USA

Bonine   use as directed on
Dramamine   the label
Marezine

Explanation

The motion of the boat disturbs the normal equilibrium of the inner ear, producing a sensation of instability. This is intensified by the visual perception of movement and the irritation of food rolling in the digestive tract. Another important factor is expectation, the psychological fear of becoming sick, which sometimes creates its own self-fulfilling prophesy. To the extent that seasickness is psychosomatic, it can sometimes be staved off by giving the victim something important to do *on deck*.

Nine out of ten people are likely to become seasick.

Those most susceptible are:
Women.
Children aged 2–10.
The thin.
The anemic.
The nervous.
The overweight.

Those nearly immune are:
The old.
The very young.
The deaf.

Prevention

The equilibrium of the inner ear can be trained. A few exercises, done morning and evening, several days before a voyage can be surprisingly helpful.

1 – Stand with your feet wide apart and sway your body in a circular motion for 5–10 minutes.

2 – Practice rolling your eyes in imitation of the boat's movement for several minutes at a time. If this produces slight nausea, stop until it passes, then continue.

Seiches

Immediately, prepare for a tidal-like change in water level of up to 7ft. (2 meters).

See: Aground, Chafe, Drying out, fenders

This change can occur at intervals of from a few minutes up to several hours.

Seiches do *not* forecast a coming storm. Rather, they are the result of the passing of a depression. Generally, they are seasonal – often only in the spring – and localized, for example, the western Spanish coast and the Great Lakes.

Self-steering

Sheet-to-tiller gear

Nearly any boat can be made to steer herself, on nearly any course, by a sheet-to-tiller arrangement. Some experimentation will, of course, be necessary.

Principle

Some part of the running rigging is led to the helm to pull it to windward. This pull should increase when the boat luffs, and slacken when the boat bears away. When the weather helm is more than is necessary, it can be balanced by an elastic.

The sheet should pull to windward.

The elastic should pull to leeward.

The elastic should be slack when the rudder is amidships.

NOTE:

Any sail or course change will require an adjustment of the system, and this may entail shifting from one method to another.

To windward

Elastic or rubber tubing supplies weather
helm ■ **344, 345.**

On a broad reach

Foresail control ■ **346, 347.**

In light winds

Main boom control. ■ 348.

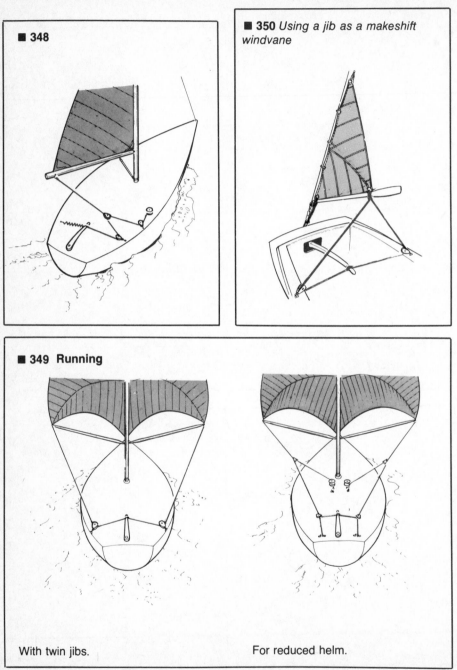

■ 348

■ 350 *Using a jib as a makeshift windvane*

■ 349 Running

With twin jibs.

For reduced helm.

When the wind is abaft the beam

A small jib can be hanked on the backstay.

A spar or oar is tied along the foot of the sail and one end lashed or shackled to the backstay.

Lines tied to the clew are run through blocks on either side of the cockpit and then to the tiller.

WARNING:

Should the boat jibe, the sail will foul the main boom.

Semaphore

Sextant

■ **351 352** *Checking the perpendicular alignment of the Index Arm Mirror*

Mirror adjustment

Principle

The two mirrors, the Index Arm Mirror and the Horizon Mirror, must be correctly aligned for an accurate reflection of the sun.

The center of the face of the Horizon Mirror must be at an angle of 45 degrees to a base line running from the center of the eyepiece to the center of the mirror.

The center of the Index Arm Mirror must be directly over the point of pivot, and the face of the mirror along a line from the pivot to the zero point on the scale.

Both mirrors must be at an angle of 90 degrees to the face of the sextant.

Procedure

To check the perpendicular alignment of the Index Arm Mirror ■ **351, 352**

Hold the sextant flat side up.

Set the Index Arm at about 35 degrees.

Look at the Index Arm Mirror. If the arc reflected in the mirror, and the arc behind it are a continuous line, then the mirror is perpendicular.

If there is a break in the line, then the mirror must be adjusted by the screws on the reverse side.

To check the perpendicular aligment of the Horizon Mirror ■ 353

Hold the sextant in the normal fashion.

Set the Index Arm at zero.

Sight the horizon, and adjust the micrometer so that the half in the clear side and the half on the silvered side meet.

Turn the sextant to about 45 degrees.

If the horizon line does *not* break, the mirror is in adjustment.

If the line separates, the mirror should be adjusted by the screws on the reverse side.

Index Error are plus or minus 8 minutes. Past that point the mirrors should be adjusted.

Procedure

Set the Index Arm at exactly zero.

Sight the horizon.

Adjust the arm until the two halves of the horizon meet – the half reflected from the Index Mirror and the one sighted through the clear portion of the Horizon Mirror ■ 354.

Record the angle:
If it is negative – below the zero mark – the Index Error must be added.
If it is positive – above the zero mark – the Index Error must be subtracted.

■ **353** *Checking the perpendicular alignment of the Horizon Mirror*

■ **354** *Finding the Index Error*

Index Error

Principle

The two sextant mirrors need *not* be in perfect vertical alignment to each other. A small error can be tolerated and most sextants have one. However, it must be known and included in the calculation of a sight. The generally accepted limits for

Cleaning

Should the sextant become immersed in salt water or coated with spray, it should be carefully rinsed and cleaned with fresh water, dried and the joints oiled with a light machine oil.

Longitude without a sextant – Meridian Passage by Horizon Sight

Prerequisites

A clear sunrise followed by a clear sunset, though rare. A crude cross-staff can be easily improvised instead. Protect your eyes by filtering the sun's rays through smoked glass or light cloth.

GMT.

The date. If this is not known, an approximation to within two days will cause a possible error of 15 minutes of longitude, no more than 15 nautical miles.

The Nautical Almanac

Principle

Longitude is nearly synonymous with Time as both are used to measure the eastward or westward distance from the Greenwich meridian. 360 degrees Longitude, or the distance around the world, equals 24 hours. 180 degrees equals 12 hours, and 1 degree equals four minutes. **See: Time** for an Arc (Longitude) to Time conversion table.

Therefore, if you know the precise instant the sun crosses your meridian – that is, passes directly overhead – by simple subtraction you can find the difference (in Time) between your Meridian Passage and the one at Greenwich which is listed in *The Nautical Almanac*. That figure, in Time (hours and minutes), can be converted easily into Arc (degrees and minutes) and so become Longitude.

Procedure

Record in GMT the exact moment of sunrise: when the sun's lower limb touches the horizon.

On the same day record the moment of sunset, again when the sun's lower limb touches the horizon.

Compute the elapsed time between sunrise and sunset, then divide it by two.

That figure, in hours and minutes, when added to the moment of sunrise is the instant the sun was directly overhead – it's Meridian Passage.

In *The Nautical Almanac*, under the correct date, in the lower right-hand corner of the right-hand page is the time of Meridian Passage at Greenwich.

Compute the difference – in Time – between your moment of Meridian Passage and the one at Greenwich.

Convert that Time (hours and minutes) into Arc (degrees and minutes) which is Longitude.

See: Time – Table for the Conversion of Arc (Longitude) to Time (page 230).

A Sun Sight without a sextant

Prerequisites

A clear sunrise or sunset.

The date.

GMT.

The Nautical Almanac.

Sight Reduction Tables – but *not* HO 214 (HD 486) which does not tabulate below five degrees of Altitude.

Principle

Theoretically, a Sun Sight can be taken at any time during the day when it can be observed clearly. Twice during the day it is possible to know the sun's position in the sky without the aid of a sextant.

At sunrise and sunset, even with the naked eye, one can record the instant the lower limb touches the horizon. The 'observed altitude' becomes 0 degrees, and the sight can then be worked out in the normal fashion. A horizon sight will not be as accurate as one taken above 10 degrees and will require additional corrections, nonetheless, if carefully observed and calculated, it can provide a reliable position line.

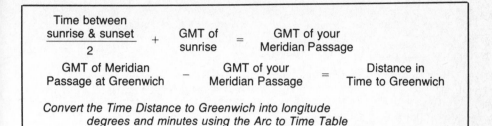

$$\frac{\text{Time between sunrise \& sunset}}{2} + \frac{\text{GMT of}}{\text{sunrise}} = \frac{\text{GMT of your}}{\text{Meridian Passage}}$$

$$\frac{\text{GMT of Meridian}}{\text{Passage at Greenwich}} - \frac{\text{GMT of your}}{\text{Meridian Passage}} = \frac{\text{Distance in}}{\text{Time to Greenwich}}$$

Convert the Time Distance to Greenwich into longitude degrees and minutes using the Arc to Time Table

Procedure

Using either the naked eye or a pair of binoculars, watch the sun until its lower limb touches the horizon.

WARNING:

Use a protective shade. If one is not available, a piece of glass held over a candle for a few moments or a dark strip of photographic film will make a good substitute.

Record the time for the passage of both the upper and lower limbs. Although only one is necessary, two sights always provide a partial check.

Compute the sight in the normal fashion using Sight Reduction Tables, *except*:

1 – When correcting – subtracting – for refraction, use an Apparent Altitude of 0 degrees.
  For the sun, this is:
  Upper limb $-50.3'$
  Lower limb $-18.3'$
  For stars and planets $-34.5'$

2 – Additional corrections must be made for temperature and barometric pressure. **See: Time** for a table for barometric and temperature corrections of a Horizon Sight (page 229).

Your course without a sextant

Prerequisites

A clear night.

The date – an approximation is sufficient.

The Nautical Almanac.

GMT

An accurate compass.

A Star Finder – the one in *The Nautical Almanac* will suffice.

Principle

Every heavenly body has its 'ground point', or Geographic Position, the point on earth which is directly beneath it. Obviously, this changes from moment to moment, but if you can find a star which will pass directly over your destination and know precisely at what time this will occur, then a bearing from you to the star at that instant will be your course. It is often called 'The Star of Bethlehem principle'.

The celestial coordinates are analogous to those of the earth. Instead of Latitude a star is given a Declination, and for 57 stars these Declinations are listed on the

---

Horizon Sight

$$\frac{\text{Observed altitude}}{\text{0 degrees}} - \text{The Dip} - 18.3' \pm \frac{\text{Corrections for}}{\text{Temperature \&}} = \frac{\text{True}}{\text{Altitude}}$$
lower limb   Barometric
                                                    Pressure

left pages of *The Nautical Almanac* under the heading 'Stars – Dec'.

If you select a star whose declination is roughly the same as the Latitude of your destination, then at some point in time that star must have its 'ground point' at or near to that of your destination.

When this occurs is dependent on its Longitude, which is computed from its Sidereal Hour Angle (listed in the column under 'SHA') *plus* the Greenwich Hour Angle of Aries – which is given on the left side of the page. At the moment these two figures total your Longitude, the star is directly above your destination.

Procedure

For the appropriate date in *The Nautical Almanac*, read down the list of stars under the column 'Stars – Dec' until you find a star with approximately the same declination as the latitude of your destination.

Record the Sidereal Hour Angle listed in the adjacent column, then *subtract* it from the longitude of your destination.

If the longitude of your destination is smaller than the Sidereal Hour Angle of the star, *add* 360 to your Longitude.

If the longitude of your destination is an easterly one, *subtract* it first from 360.

The result is the GHA – Greenwich Hour Angle – of Aries. Match that position with the time – shown in GMT – in the adjacent column, and at that moment the star is above your destination.

Locate the star with a Star Finder or the star charts in *The Nautical Almanac*. **See: Stars**

At the proper moment, sight the star over an accurate compass.

The bearing is your course.

A makeshift sextant

Materials

One piece of plywood or hardboard.

Two pieces of mirror – approximately $\frac{3}{4} \times 1\frac{1}{4}$in. (2×3cm.), each with a minimum of one straight edge.

Two wooden blocks – approximately $\frac{3}{4} \times 1\frac{1}{4}$in. (2×3cm.).

Two or three 2in. (5cm.) strips of darkened photographic film, preferably the leader of a developed roll, or strips of dark plastic bag.

One empty 35mm. film container, or an equal sized plastic bottle.

One drawer handle.

Five screws.

8in. (20cm.) dark-colored thread.

Procedure

Drill the hole for the Index Arm pivot
■ **358.**

Using the template, cut the Index Arm from another piece of wood.

Drill a hole in the center of each of the two blocks, and glue a mirror to one side. These will become the Index and Horizon Mirrors.

Drill a small hole – pencil lead size – in

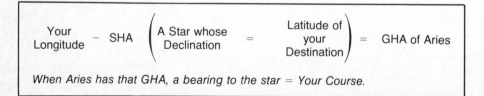

Your Longitude − SHA (A Star whose Declination = Latitude of your Destination) = GHA of Aries

When Aries has that GHA, a bearing to the star = Your Course.

Constructing a makeshift sextant

■ **355**

■ **356**

■ **357**

■ **358**

the center of the film container bottom, then glue it in place with its horizontal axis along the line ■ **355.**

Mount the Horizon Mirror ■ **356** with its *face* along the *45-degree angle* and its axis at point ■ **357.**

Mount the Index Mirror with its *face* over the *center* of the Index Arm pivot ■ **358.**

Attach the Index Arm with a large screw, and tie one end of the thread around the screw. Glue or tie the other end to the lower tip of the Index Arm so that the thread passes the zero point on the compass rose and the zero point on the scale.

Mount the handle on the back.

Bend the film into slides or cut the plastic into strips and put as many as necessary over the mirrors. Tie in place with rubber bands or string.

Adjust the Index Error by slightly changing the position of the thread.

NOTE:

The hole on the Index Mirror block should be slightly larger than the screw to allow for Index Error adjustment when the sextant is completed.

Each mirror must be mounted at exactly 90 degrees to the surface of the sextant.

Sharks

If someone is in the water

A number of researchers report that noise will frighten sharks away:

1 – Start the engine.
2 – Beat on the hull.
3 – Fire a rifle into the water.

For the swimmer

Shout into the water.

Beat on diving tanks.

If spear fishing, release any catch.

Face the shark and swim slowly back to the boat.

WARNING:

Do not urinate if a shark is nearby. When a shark attacks, he first dives then turns on his back. This means that as long as you can see the dorsal fin you are safe.

NOTE:

Wearing clothing in the water appears to offer some protection in that sharks are *more likely* to be attracted to a naked swimmer than a fully dressed one.

If attacked

'Quiet aggression' is the best tactic.

Sharks will generally test their prey (hitting it with their nose or body) before striking. When they do, they should be struck forcefully with either hands or feet.

A hasty retreat can be very dangerous, as it is senseless to try to outswim a shark.

Shoals and sandbars

See also: Aground, drying out

When wind and tide are in the same direction

A smooth slick will probably indicate deeper water.

When wind and tide are in contrary directions

Rough wavelets will probably indicate deeper water.

If caught on shoals

Do *not* try to ride the backs of waves.

If under power:

If the stern 'falls', the boat is climbing the back of the wave ahead; throttle back.

If the bow 'falls', the wave astern is overtaking the boat; accelerate.

WARNING:

Never tow a dinghy over a bar. It could easily fill with water, sink, and act as a powerful sea anchor.

Sharks that are known to be dangerous

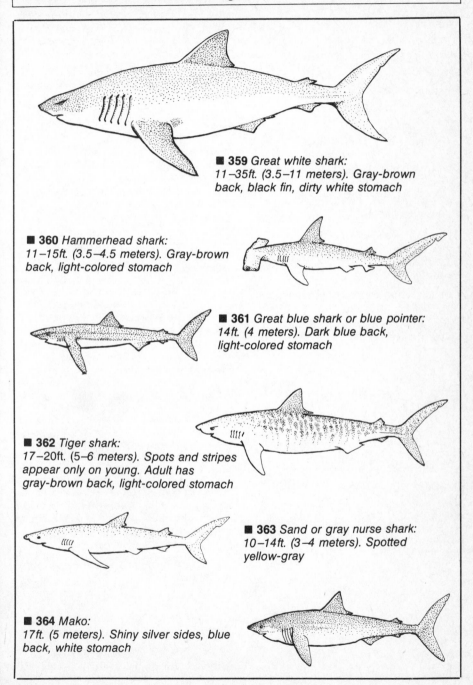

■ **359** *Great white shark: 11–35ft. (3.5–11 meters). Gray-brown back, black fin, dirty white stomach*

■ **360** *Hammerhead shark: 11–15ft. (3.5–4.5 meters). Gray-brown back, light-colored stomach*

■ **361** *Great blue shark or blue pointer: 14ft. (4 meters). Dark blue back, light-colored stomach*

■ **362** *Tiger shark: 17–20ft. (5–6 meters). Spots and stripes appear only on young. Adult has gray-brown back, light-colored stomach*

■ **363** *Sand or gray nurse shark: 10–14ft. (3–4 meters). Spotted yellow-gray*

■ **364** *Mako: 17ft. (5 meters). Shiny silver sides, blue back, white stomach*

Shock

Symptoms

Can accompany any serious injury or illness, seasickness included.

Person becomes cold, pale, sweaty and extremely weak.

Fainting will probably occur.

Treatment

Immediate rest, with the feet slightly elevated above the head.

Warmth.

If the person is conscious

A hot drink – but *no alcohol.*

If the person is unconscious and not breathing

Immediately begin mouth-to-mouth resuscitation.

See: Artificial respiration

Shrouds

See: Rigging failures

Sight Reduction Tables

Finding longitude without Sight Reduction Tables

Prerequisites

A sextant.

The Nautical Almanac.

GMT.

The date.

Principle

Longitude and time are virtually synonymous – 360 degrees of longitude equals 24 hours, 1 degree equals 4 minutes. Therefore, if one is known, the other can be calculated quickly. **See: Time** – Conversion of Arc (longitude) to Time.

If one can determine the precise moment, in hours, minutes and seconds, when the sun passes directly overhead, that is, the instant of Meridian Passage, then the difference between that Meridian Passage and the one at Greenwich, which is given in *The Nautical Almanac*, can easily be found by addition or subtraction. This difference in Time can then be converted into longitude and marked off from the Greenwich Meridian.

The complication is that of knowing exactly when the sun is directly overhead, since the sun often remains several minutes at its apex. However, one can choose a Time earlier and later in the day when the sun's movement is more rapid. By carefully measuring the elapsed time between two points, one in the morning and the other in the afternoon, when the sun's elevation above the horizon is the same, and dividing by two, Meridian Passage can be accurately determined.

Procedure

Take a morning sun sight 10–15 minutes before the approximate time of Meridian Passage and carefully note the sextant reading and the GMT in hours, minutes and seconds.

After Meridian Passage, in the afternoon, follow the sun on its downwards arc until it reaches the precise angle of your morning sight. Again carefully note the time in hours, minutes and seconds.

Calculate the elapsed time between the two sights.

Divide it by two.

Add the result to the time of your morning sight.

The answer is the time of Meridian Passage, that is, the moment the sun crossed your meridian. Next, find the time

GMT of afternoon sight − GMT of morning sight (same elevation)

$$\frac{\text{GMT of afternoon sight} - \text{GMT of morning sight (same elevation)}}{2} + \text{GMT of morning sight} = \text{GMT of your Meridian Passage}$$

$$\text{GMT of Meridian Passage at Greenwich} - \text{GMT of your Meridian Passage} = \text{Distance in Time to Greenwich}$$

Convert the Time distance to Greenwich into longitude degrees and minutes using the Arc to Time Table (page 230).

of Meridian Passage at Greenwich. This is given in *The Nautical Almanac*, under the appropriate date, on the right-hand pages, in the lower right-hand corner under the heading 'Sun – Mer. Pass'.

Calculate the difference in Time between your Meridian Passage and the one at Greenwich. Convert that Time difference into longitude **See: Time** – Conversion of Arc (longitude) to Time. The result is your longitude, to be marked off east or west, depending upon your position relative to the Greenwich Meridian.

Finding latitude without Sight Reduction Tables

Prerequisites

A sextant.

The date.

The Nautical Almanac.

Approximate time in GMT.

Principle

At local noon, your noon, when the sun is directly overhead, a position line drawn at right angles to the sun's bearing would be along an east-west axis, that is, on a latitude. Twice during the year – at solstice – the sun's angle at that moment would equal latitude. At other times one must add or subtract the sun's Declination, that is, its 'latitude in the heavens'.

Procedure

Sight the sun in the late morning, and follow it as it rises. Record its highest altitude.

Find the right-hand page in *The Nautical Almanac* for the appropriate date. (These pages list the sun's Declination in degrees and minutes for every hour of the year under the heading – 'Sun – Dec.') Using the time to the nearest hour – in GMT – record the sun's Declination, its direction – north or south indicated by N or S – and angle in degrees and minutes.

If the direction and your hemisphere are the *same, add* the Declination to the sun's Altitude to find your latitude.

If the direction and your hemisphere are *different* (contrary, that is, one north, the other, south), *subtract* the declination from the sun's Altitude to find your latitude.

$$\text{Altitude of the Sun at Meridian Passage} \pm \text{Sun's Declination at that time in GMT} = \text{Your Latitude}$$

NOTE:

The sun often appears to 'sit' at its apex for a few moments before beginning its descent.

Signal mirror

See: Heliograph

Sleeping pills

	DOSAGE Weak
England Valium	10mg.
	Strong
Amylobarbitone	1–2 100mg. tablets
	Weak
France Valium	10mg.
	Strong
Mogadan	1–2 5mg. tablets
	Weak
Germany Valium	10mg.
	Strong
Nembutal	1–2 100mg. tablets
	Weak
U.S. Valium	10mg.
	Strong
Nembutal	1–2 100mg. tablets

NOTE:

If a person has sustained a serious injury (except head injury) at sea, it is easier on the crew and the injured man if he is kept under sedation until arrival in port.
Weak
Dosage

WARNING:

Do not administer these drugs more than four times a day.

Solar still

See also: Distillation, Water

Materials ■ 365

A large, wide-mouthed pot or tin.

A few rags.

A glass or bowl.

A sheet of plastic, preferably dark in color.

■ 365 *A makeshift solar still*

Procedure

Place the glass in the center of the pot and lay the rags around it.

Fill the pot $\frac{1}{4}$ to $\frac{1}{3}$ full with salt water.

Tie the plastic sheet over the pot and put a weight, such as a stone or shackle, in the middle of it.

Put the pot in the sun.

Principle

The sun's heat will cause the water to evaporate and condense on the plastic sheet where it will run down to the center and drip into the glass.

Sound signals

See: Fog

Spanish reef

An emergency reef to replace a small foresail or ease the strain on a damaged head:

An ordinary overhand knot at the head will make a small reduction.

A larger reduction should be made with a figure eight knot.

■ **366** *A Spanish reef*

NOTE:

Canvas sails may be stretched and damaged in this manner. Modern Dacron/luff sails are hardly affected, but a wire may be damaged in the knot.

Spanish windlass

Purpose ■ 367

Whenever more leverage is required and a winch is either broken or unavailable.

■ **367** *A Spanish windlass*

Procedure

A spar, preferably one of sizable diameter, is lodged against the mast. A loose lashing may be necessary to prevent it from sliding off.

One person holds the outer end, while a second winds the line around the spar, taking a turn at a time with a large screwdriver or lever of some kind.

Speedometer

See: Log

Sprains

Treatment

Limit the activity of the limb.

Elevate it to reduce swelling and pain.

Apply cold salt water compresses for the first 24 hours, then hot ones.

If necessary, bind the joint for support. When binding a sprain always begin at the furthest point on the extremity and bind toward the body.

Stars

The North, or Pole, Star ■ 368

A line drawn from Merak to Dubhe, the two outer stars of the Plow (Big Dipper, or Great Bear), and extended *five times* will reach the North Star.

NOTE:

When looking for the Plow, remember that it occupies about 40 degrees in the sky.

See: Distance-off – natural hand angles (page 65)

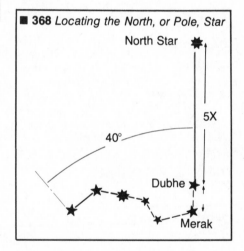

■ **368** *Locating the North, or Pole, Star*

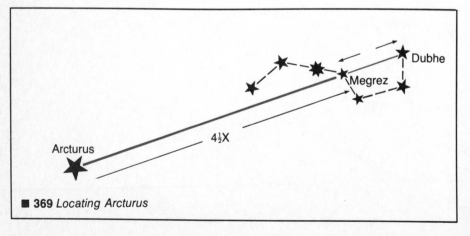

■ **369** *Locating Arcturus*

Locating other navigational stars from the Plow

Arcturus ■ 369

A line drawn from Dubhe to Megrez and extended $4\frac{1}{2}$ *times* will reach Arcturus.

Vega ■ 370

Draw a line from Alkaid, the last star on the Plow's handle to the North Star. Another line taken from its mid-point and drawn perpendicular, $1\frac{1}{5}$ *times* as long as the first line, will reach Vega.

Altair ■ 371

Complete the triangle used to find Vega by drawing a hypotenuse from Alkaid to Vega. Extend that line by $^2/_3$ and it will reach Altair.

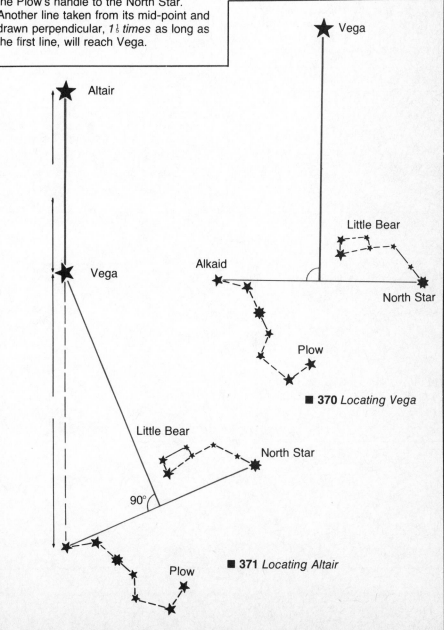

■ 370 *Locating Vega*

■ 371 *Locating Altair*

Capella ■ 372

Draw a line across the Plow's two pointers – Merak and Dubhe – to the North Star. Draw a second line perpendicular to it, extend it until it is 1 ¹/₃ the distance from Dubhe to the North Star and it will reach Capella.

Deneb ■ 373 (opposite)

Draw a line from Phecda to Megrez, the two inner stars of the Plow, and extend it to the tip of the Little Bear. Double the distance and it will reach Deneb.

Steel hull repair

Leaks

A small crack or hole can be filled with mastic, filler, cold solder, fiberglass or epoxy resin.

Holes

METHOD 1   A riveted steel or metal patch

See: Aluminum repair

METHOD 2   A fiberglass patch

See: Fiberglass repair

Sterilization

See also: Antiseptics

In emergency conditions, it is impossible to sterilize an implement such as a knife or a sewing needle fully. However, partial sterilization can be achieved by:

Boiling the object for at least 20 minutes.

Heating it over a flame for two minutes.

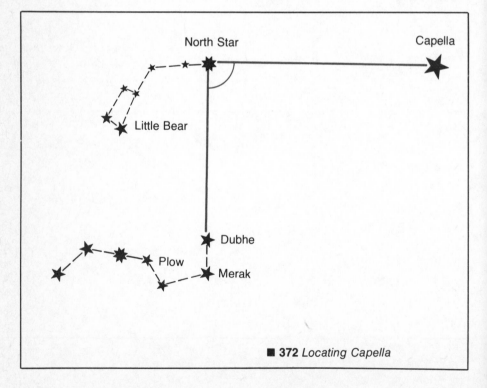

■ 372 *Locating Capella*

Soaking it in a solution of 1 cup bleach and 1 quart (1 liter) of water.

Soaking it in alcohol – at least a 70% solution.

NOTE:

After the implement is sterilized be sure that only other sterilized materials come in contact with it.

Stop

International code of signals

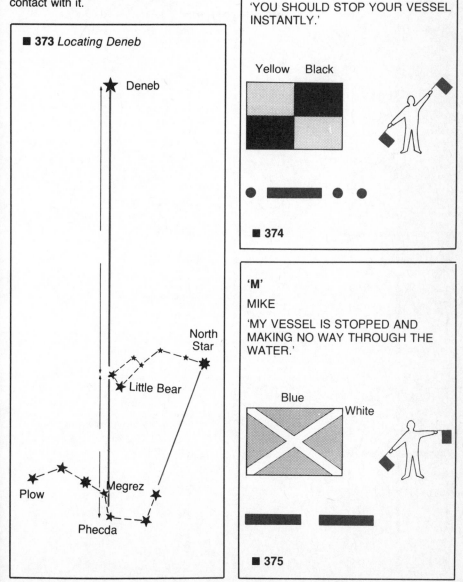

■ **373** *Locating Deneb*

'L'

LIMA

'YOU SHOULD STOP YOUR VESSEL INSTANTLY.'

Yellow   Black

■ **374**

'M'

MIKE

'MY VESSEL IS STOPPED AND MAKING NO WAY THROUGH THE WATER.'

Blue   White

■ **375**

Storm-warning signals

Day

Night

Meaning

Strong wind – near gale, Beaufort 6–7. Will be taken down if the wind abates in six hours.

White

Green

Meaning

Gale or storm expected commencing in the NW quadrant.

Red

Red

Meaning

Gale or storm expected commencing in the SW quadrant.

White

White

International system of visual storm-warning signals

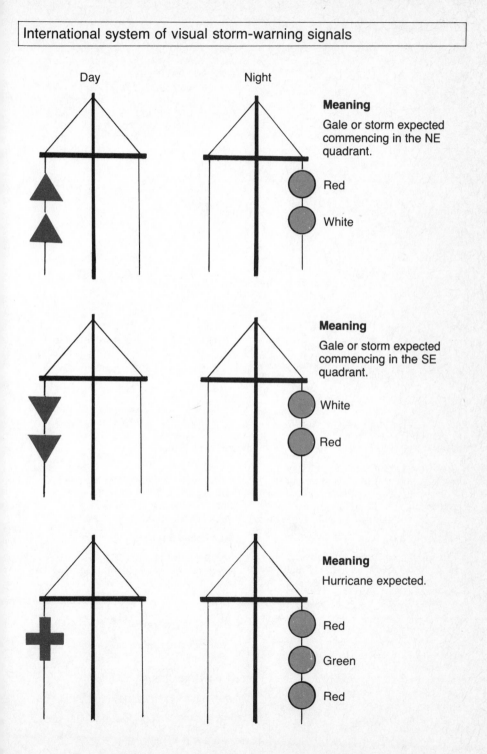

Day   Night

Meaning

Gale or storm expected commencing in the NE quadrant.

Red

White

Meaning

Gale or storm expected commencing in the SE quadrant.

White

Red

Meaning

Hurricane expected.

Red

Green

Red

During daytime *flags* may be shown

One flag – white or red: Wind expected to veer.

Two flags – white or red: Wind expected to back.

NOTE:

Many countries have national or local visual storm-warning signals which are displayed in conjunction with the international ones. These signals are described in the appropriate volumes of the sailing directions.

Small craft, Gale, Storm and Hurricane warnings

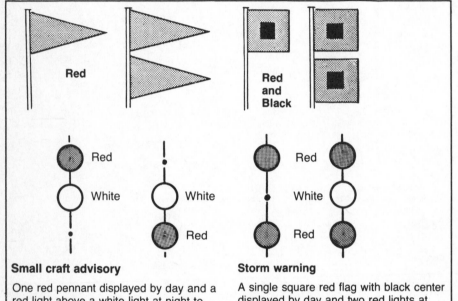

Small craft advisory

One red pennant displayed by day and a red light above a white light at night to indicate winds up to 38 mph (33 knots) and/or sea conditions dangerous to small craft operations are forecast for the area.

Gale warning

Two red pennants displayed by day and a white light above a red light at night to indicate winds ranging from 39 to 54 mph (34 to 47 knots) are forecast.

Storm warning

A single square red flag with black center displayed by day and two red lights at night to indicate winds 55 mph (48 knots) and above *(no matter how high the velocity)* are forecast for the area.

Hurricane Warning

Two square red flags with black center displayed by day and one white and two red lights by night.

Stormsails

Trysail ■ 376

The sail area should be smaller than a reefed-down mainsail. It can be hoisted on all points of sailing.

Rigging a trysail

Lash the boom amidships (in its crutch, if possible).

Take down the mainsail.

Bend the trysail to the mast.

Hoist the trysail on the main halyard.

■ 376 *Sheeting a trysail*

Sheeting a Trysail

METHOD 1

If the boom is short, the trysail can be sheeted like a jib, with a sheet to each side run through a block well aft. This method of sheeting is preferable when there is a danger of jibing.

It can be done even when the boom is long by giving weather sheet slack to pass over boom. Tacking is easy.

METHOD 2

The trysail is sheeted to the end of the boom and can be trimmed by the mainsheet. This method of sheeting makes it easier to tack.

A makeshift trysail

A jib as a trysail

METHOD 1 ■ 377, 378, 379

The sail foot is placed against the mast. To fit properly, the foot must be reinforced, either by sewing hooks to the bolt rope which can be clipped to the sail slides (though in violent weather other lines tend to get caught inside the clips, which could prevent the sail from being lowered), or by cutting eyelets and passing lines around the mast secured by toggles.

■ 377 *The jib as a trysail*

■ 378   **■ 379**

METHOD 2 ■ 380

Lash the tack around the gooseneck. A pennant may be needed here ■ 380A.

Pass a bight of line through the head and around the mast ■ 380B.

Tighten the luff with a halyard winch.

Sheet the clew to the end of the boom or to a block on the quarter. ■ 380C.

If the leech is slack, bouse the sheet down at the proper angle to the boom. Use the mainsheet to control the boom ■ 380D.

■ 380 *The jib as a trysail*

Jibs

As a general rule, a working jib takes up approximately 75% of the fore-triangle. A storm jib should take up only about 40%. Its luff should not overlap the mast. Its foot should be cut high, so that it won't be vulnerable to oncoming waves.

A makeshift storm jib ■ 381

The Dacron material of a storm sail is the same as that of a set of working sails. Hence, to serve as a storm jib, a normal jib need only be reefed. A set of points and eyelets can be sewn in and cringles positioned for a new tack and clew.

Set on a short tack pennant to keep it out of the water.

Streaming a warp

See: Heaving to

Submarines

Submarines, including pleasure craft, are not required to give signals, and no warning is required when surfacing. Equipment is available for large and small craft alike, which indicates if other vessels are above.

Federal lighting requirements are the same as for any vessel in the water. Basically, submarines must have red and green starboard lights and display white lights. Submarine lights, including a flashing amber light, are also required. The states, which have control over fresh water lakes, can implement these federal regulations, so requirements can vary from state to state.

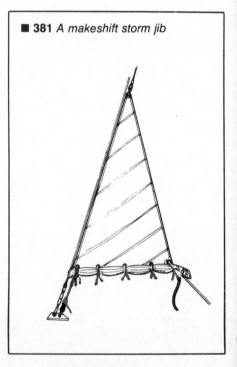

■ 381 *A makeshift storm jib*

Sunburn

See also: Burns, Heat exhaustion, Sunstroke

Treatment

If severe

Treat as a burn. **See: Burns**

If accompanied by chills, fever and/or swelling:

Apply cool compresses of:

Three tablespoons vinegar and one quart or liter fresh water

or

Three tablespoons baking soda (sodium bicarbonate) and one quart or liter fresh water

or

One tablespoon Epsom salts (magnesium sulphate) and one quart or liter fresh water.

Drink plenty of fluids – at least one quart or liter every three hours.

Take vitamin C – 1gm. per hour for the first six hours.

NOTE:

If suntan lotion is not available, olive oil, coconut oil, or simply cooking oil mixed with a few drops of iodine can be used to screen the sun's rays.

Sunstroke

See also: Heat exhaustion

Symptoms

Usually occurs after vigorous exercise.

Skin is dry, flushed and hot.

Confusion.

Dizziness.

Loss of consciousness.

NOTE:

By contrast, in a condition of *heat exhaustion*, the skin is pale and moist.

Treatment

Immediately lower the victim's body temperature

Place him in the shade and fan him.

Put him in a tub of cool water.

Sponge or throw water on him.

NOTE:

Sunstroke is essentially a total collapse of the body's heat regulation system. Without immediate treatment, body temperature will continue to rise and cause either death or brain damage.

Massage the skin to stimulate circulation.

When conscious, the victim should immediately drink cool liquids.

Recovery will be slow and require at least 48 hours.

T

Tackle

See: Block and tackle

Temperature

See: Weather forecast

Tiller

If the tiller fitting is damaged or broken

Lash a boathook or oars to either side ■ 382.

or

Steer the boat without a tiller ■ 383.

Drill a hole in the rudder blade near the waterline. Pass lines through the hole, knot them in place then run them back to the cockpit.

or

Screw, bolt or nail a fitting of any kind to the rudder blade near the waterline. Connect two lines and run them back through blocks to the cockpit winches.

Don't forget the vise grip pliers as the basis for a makeshift. Carry an emergency tiller with fitting.

NOTE:

It is possible to steer by sail trimming and weight shifting with the leeline free.

To lash a tiller ■ 384

Only one end should be securely lashed down. The other end must be instantly releasable.

■ **382** *Replacing a broken tiller*

To repair a broken tiller

Break a boathook in half and thrust the ends into the fitting.

Or use an oar, or piece of a jib boom.

This can be reinforced by lashing to it:
A large screwdriver.
Bolts, pipe or a bottle screw.
Pieces of floorboard.
Vise grips or a monkey wrench.

■ **383** *Steering without a tiller*

■ **384** *Lashing down the tiller with a quick release*

Time

Stations that transmit time signals:

Place	Call Sign	Frequencies (MHz)
Buenos Aires (Argentina)	LOL	5, 10, 15
Shanghai (China)	BPV	5, 10, 15
Liblice (Czechoslovakia)	OMA	2.5
Chevannes (France)	FFH	2.5
Kihei (Hawaii)	WWVH	2.5, 5, 10, 15
New Delhi (India)	ATA	10
Turin Rome (Italy)	IBF IAM	5 5
Tokyo (Japan)	JJY	2.5, 5, 10, 15
Johannesburg (South Africa)	ZUO	10
Rugby (U.K.)	MSF	2.5, 5, 10
Ft. Collins, Colorado (U.S.A.)	WWV	2.5, 5, 10, 15, 20, 25
Moscow (U.S.S.R.)	RWM	2.5, 5, 10, 15
Ottawa (Canada)	CHU	3.33, 7.335, 14.67

To find GMT by a sunrise or sunset sight

Use this procedure only if you have no sextant and you know your position.

Principle

Latitude can easily be found without an accurate knowledge of Time. **See: Sight Reduction Tables** – *Latitude by 'Noon Sight'* (page 213).

In computing a normal sight, an error of one minute in time can affect your longitude by as much as 15 minutes, but it will hardly change a position line which runs east-west, that is, longitudinally. If latitude is known and remains constant, any error will be in terms of longitude, which can easily be converted to Time. **See:** *Table for Conversion of Arc (Longitude) to Time* (page 230).

Prerequisites

A clear sunrise or sunset.

Date.

An estimate of GMT.

The Nautical Almanac.

Sight Reduction Tables – but not HO 214 (HD 486) which does not tabulate below five degrees of altitude.

Your latitude.

Procedure

Using either the naked eye or a pair of binoculars, watch the sun until the lower limb touches the horizon.

Record the time of passage with your best estimation of GMT

Compute the sight in the normal fashion, *except*:

Correct for an Apparent Altitude of 0 degrees:
Upper Limb − 50.3′
Lower Limb − 18.3′

Correct for temperature and barometric pressure. **See: Time** – *Table for Barometric and Temperature Corrections of a Horizon Sight* (page 209).

Plot the position line.

Measure the latitudinal distance – that is, on a north-south line from your Assumed Position to your Position Line.

Convert that distance from degrees and minutes into Time – minutes and seconds by the *Conversion of Arc (Longitude) to Time Table* (page 230).

That is the chronometric error.

If your true position is *eastwards* of your Assumed position, the watch is *fast; if westwards, slow.*

WARNING:

Use a protective filter of some kind. If one is not available, a piece of smoked glass or photographic film will make a good substitute.

Table for barometric and temperature corrections of a horizon sight

Toothache

If tooth is sensitive to heat and percussion and relieved by cold, you have a tooth abscess. Remove any loose filling and leave open. Take pain killer. **See: Pain killers.** If swelling results, take antibiotics. **See: Antibiotics.**

If tooth is sensitive to heat and cold, check for loose or missings fillings. Clean out cavity as well as possible. Dry and place a bit of wax or well-chewed gum in the cavity.

If tooth is sore and gum adjacent to tooth is swollen, you may have periodontal or gum abscess. Treat by finger massage of swollen area, warm salt-water rinses, and good oral hygiene. If swelling persists, take antibiotics. Use pain killer as necessary.

If you have swollen bleeding gums, you may have Vincent's infection, or trench mouth. Brush teeth as well as possible. Soften toothbrush with warm water. Take antibiotics. Rinse with peroxide.

If you have tooth traumatized from a blow, straighten the tooth so you don't interfere with the bite. In most cases it will renew itself.

If the upper back teeth ache, especially when you lie down, you may have a sinus infection. Take antibiotics, cold tablets, and pain killers as necessary.

Table for Barometric and Temperature Corrections of a Horizon Sight

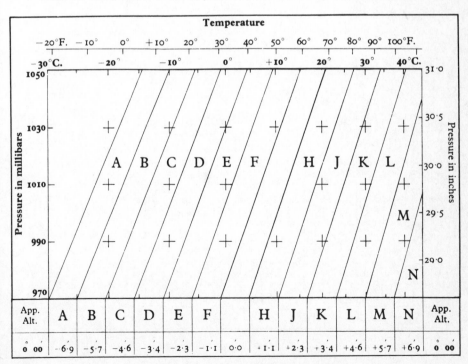

Conversion of Arc (Longitude) to Time

0°–59°		60°–119°		120°–179°		180°–239°		240°–299°		300°–359°			0′·00	0′·25	0′·50	0′·75
°	h m	°	h m	°	h m	°	h m	°	h m	°	h m	′	m s	m s	m s	m s
0	0 00	60	4 00	120	8 00	180	12 00	240	16 00	300	20 00	0	0 00	0 01	0 02	0 03
1	0 04	61	4 04	121	8 04	181	12 04	241	16 04	301	20 04	1	0 04	0 05	0 06	0 07
2	0 08	62	4 08	122	8 08	182	12 08	242	16 08	302	20 08	2	0 08	0 09	0 10	0 11
3	0 12	63	4 12	123	8 12	183	12 12	243	16 12	303	20 12	3	0 12	0 13	0 14	0 15
4	0 16	64	4 16	124	8 16	184	12 16	244	16 16	304	20 16	4	0 16	0 17	0 18	0 19
5	0 20	65	4 20	125	8 20	185	12 20	245	16 20	305	20 20	5	0 20	0 21	0 22	0 23
6	0 24	66	4 24	126	8 24	186	12 24	246	16 24	306	20 24	6	0 24	0 25	0 26	0 27
7	0 28	67	4 28	127	8 28	187	12 28	247	16 28	307	20 28	7	0 28	0 29	0 30	0 31
8	0 32	68	4 32	128	8 32	188	12 32	248	16 32	308	20 32	8	0 32	0 33	0 34	0 35
9	0 36	69	4 36	129	8 36	189	12 36	249	16 36	309	20 36	9	0 36	0 37	0 38	0 39
10	0 40	70	4 40	130	8 40	190	12 40	250	16 40	310	20 40	10	0 40	0 41	0 42	0 43
11	0 44	71	4 44	131	8 44	191	12 44	251	16 44	311	20 44	11	0 44	0 45	0 46	0 47
12	0 48	72	4 48	132	8 48	192	12 48	252	16 48	312	20 48	12	0 48	0 49	0 50	0 51
13	0 52	73	4 52	133	8 52	193	12 52	253	16 52	313	20 52	13	0 52	0 53	0 54	0 55
14	0 56	74	4 56	134	8 56	194	12 56	254	16 56	314	20 56	14	0 56	0 57	0 58	0 59
15	1 00	75	5 00	135	9 00	195	13 00	255	17 00	315	21 00	15	1 00	1 01	1 02	1 03
16	1 04	76	5 04	136	9 04	196	13 04	256	17 04	316	21 04	16	1 04	1 05	1 06	1 07
17	1 08	77	5 08	137	9 08	197	13 08	257	17 08	317	21 08	17	1 08	1 09	1 10	1 11
18	1 12	78	5 12	138	9 12	198	13 12	258	17 12	318	21 12	18	1 12	1 13	1 14	1 15
19	1 16	79	5 16	139	9 16	199	13 16	259	17 16	319	21 16	19	1 16	1 17	1 18	1 19
20	1 20	80	5 20	140	9 20	200	13 20	260	17 20	320	21 20	20	1 20	1 21	1 22	1 23
21	1 24	81	5 24	141	9 24	201	13 24	261	17 24	321	21 24	21	1 24	1 25	1 26	1 27
22	1 28	82	5 28	142	9 28	202	13 28	262	17 28	322	21 28	22	1 28	1 29	1 30	1 31
23	1 32	83	5 32	143	9 32	203	13 32	263	17 32	323	21 32	23	1 32	1 33	1 34	1 35
24	1 36	84	5 36	144	9 36	204	13 36	264	17 36	324	21 36	24	1 36	1 37	1 38	1 39
25	1 40	85	5 40	145	9 40	205	13 40	265	17 40	325	21 40	25	1 40	1 41	1 42	1 43
26	1 44	86	5 44	146	9 44	206	13 44	266	17 44	326	21 44	26	1 44	1 45	1 46	1 47
27	1 48	87	5 48	147	9 48	207	13 48	267	17 48	327	21 48	27	1 48	1 49	1 50	1 51
28	1 52	88	5 52	148	9 52	208	13 52	268	17 52	328	21 52	28	1 52	1 53	1 54	1 55
29	1 56	89	5 56	149	9 56	209	13 56	269	17 56	329	21 56	29	1 56	1 57	1 58	1 59
30	2 00	90	6 00	150	10 00	210	14 00	270	18 00	330	22 00	30	2 00	2 01	2 02	2 03
31	2 04	91	6 04	151	10 04	211	14 04	271	18 04	331	22 04	31	2 04	2 05	2 06	2 07
32	2 08	92	6 08	152	10 08	212	14 08	272	18 08	332	22 08	32	2 08	2 09	2 10	2 11
33	2 12	93	6 12	153	10 12	213	14 12	273	18 12	333	22 12	33	2 12	2 13	2 14	2 15
34	2 16	94	6 16	154	10 16	214	14 16	274	18 16	334	22 16	34	2 16	2 17	2 18	2 19
35	2 20	95	6 20	155	10 20	215	14 20	275	18 20	335	22 20	35	2 20	2 21	2 22	2 23
36	2 24	96	6 24	156	10 24	216	14 24	276	18 24	336	22 24	36	2 24	2 25	2 26	2 27
37	2 28	97	6 28	157	10 28	217	14 28	277	18 28	337	22 28	37	2 28	2 29	2 30	2 31
38	2 32	98	6 32	158	10 32	218	14 32	278	18 32	338	22 32	38	2 32	2 33	2 34	2 35
39	2 36	99	6 36	159	10 36	219	14 36	279	18 36	339	22 36	39	2 36	2 37	2 38	2 39
40	2 40	100	6 40	160	10 40	220	14 40	280	18 40	340	22 40	40	2 40	2 41	2 42	2 43
41	2 44	101	6 44	161	10 44	221	14 44	281	18 44	341	22 44	41	2 44	2 45	2 46	2 47
42	2 48	102	6 48	162	10 48	222	14 48	282	18 48	342	22 48	42	2 48	2 49	2 50	2 51
43	2 52	103	6 52	163	10 52	223	14 52	283	18 52	343	22 52	43	2 52	2 53	2 54	2 55
44	2 56	104	6 56	164	10 56	224	14 56	284	18 56	344	22 56	44	2 56	2 57	2 58	2 59
45	3 00	105	7 00	165	11 00	225	15 00	285	19 00	345	23 00	45	3 00	3 01	3 02	3 03
46	3 04	106	7 04	166	11 04	226	15 04	286	19 04	346	23 04	46	3 04	3 05	3 06	3 07
47	3 08	107	7 08	167	11 08	227	15 08	287	19 08	347	23 08	47	3 08	3 09	3 10	3 11
48	3 12	108	7 12	168	11 12	228	15 12	288	19 12	348	23 12	48	3 12	3 13	3 14	3 15
49	3 16	109	7 16	169	11 16	229	15 16	289	19 16	349	23 16	49	3 16	3 17	3 18	3 19
50	3 20	110	7 20	170	11 20	230	15 20	290	19 20	350	23 20	50	3 20	3 21	3 22	3 23
51	3 24	111	7 24	171	11 24	231	15 24	291	19 24	351	23 24	51	3 24	3 25	3 26	3 27
52	3 28	112	7 28	172	11 28	232	15 28	292	19 28	352	23 28	52	3 28	3 29	3 30	3 31
53	3 32	113	7 32	173	11 32	233	15 32	293	19 32	353	23 32	53	3 32	3 33	3 34	3 35
54	3 36	114	7 36	174	11 36	234	15 36	294	19 36	354	23 36	54	3 36	3 37	3 38	3 39
55	3 40	115	7 40	175	11 40	235	15 40	295	19 40	355	23 40	55	3 40	3 41	3 42	3 43
56	3 44	116	7 44	176	11 44	236	15 44	296	19 44	356	23 44	56	3 44	3 45	3 46	3 47
57	3 48	117	7 48	177	11 48	237	15 48	297	19 48	357	23 48	57	3 48	3 49	3 50	3 51
58	3 52	118	7 52	178	11 52	238	15 52	298	19 52	358	23 52	58	3 52	3 53	3 54	3 55
59	3 56	119	7 56	179	11 56	239	15 56	299	19 56	359	23 56	59	3 56	3 57	3 58	3 59

Towing

International Code of Symbols

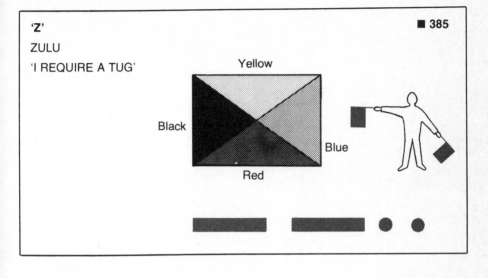

'Z'
ZULU
'I REQUIRE A TUG'

■ 385

Yellow
Black
Blue
Red

Towing signals – International Waters

By day

A diamond shape where it can best be seen, by both the tug and the tow ■ **386.**

By night

When towing, a vessel exhibits *two masthead lights* in a vertical line ■ **387.**

■ **387** *Towing signals by night*

■ **386** *Towing signals by day*

■ **388** *Towing signals by night, the tow being more than 660ft. (200 meters)*

If the tow exceeds 660ft. (200 meters) *three masthead lights* are exhibited in a vertical line ■ 388.

If the tug and tow are unable to deviate from their course, then *in addition*, the tug exhibits *red-white-red* lights in a vertical line ■ 389.

■ 389 *Towing signals by night, tug and tow being unable to deviate from course*

For towing signals when the length of the tow exceeds 660ft. (200 meters)

Note that U.S. Inland Waterway Rules differ.

> ### At sea

For the towboat

Approach the boat in need from her leeward side.

Pass alongside, turn, then throw the towline to her as you cross her bow ■ 390.

To maintain maneuverability, fasten the towline to a point *forward* of the rudder. Tugboats usually tow from a position near amidships.

A bridle can be tied between the cockpit winches ■ 391.

A harness can be lashed around the Samson post or mast ■ 392 and the bight run aft.

■ 390 *Passing the towline to the tow*

■ 391 *A towing bridle*

■ **392** *A towing harness*

NOTE:

If two warps need to be joined together, use a carrick bend. **See: Knots**

Always keep a large knife or ax ready in case the towline must be cut.

Allow plenty of scope for the towrope. It is better to err on the side of having a towrope too long than one too short.

If there is a sea running: The length of the warp should be approximately the wavelength of the sea so that both boats will ride the waves with the same rhythm ■ **393.**

A weight, such as a small anchor or several feet (a few meters) of chain, shackled to the line will act as a shock absorber.

Begin the tow *only* when the two boats and the towrope are on the same axis, that is, on a straight line.

Surge any slack in the line around a post or cleat so that the rope does not snap or jerk.

■ **393** *The length of the towline*

■ **394** *Using the anchor and anchor chain as a shock absorber*

WARNING:

Always keep tension on the towline so that it will not foul the propeller.

The towline should be boused into a bow fairlead to hold it in place securely, or be guided by a loose lashing to a bow fitting.

If no secure fitting is available, shackle the towline to the anchor or anchor chain and secure it to a strong point. In a heavy swell this can be advantageous as the anchor will act as a shock absorber ■ **394.**

NOTE:

If an agreement concerning a fee for the tow is reached, even verbally, in the presence of witnesses, this prevents a salvage claim being made later. **See: Salvage**

Legally, the two boats – the tug and the boat being towed – are regarded as one craft. The captain of the tug is in charge.

Establish a clear set of signals with the boat being towed for: *Stop, slow down, go ahead* and *release the line.* ■ **395, 396, 397, 398.**

■ **395** *'CUT! RELEASE THE LINE!'*

■ **396** *'STOP!'*

■ **397** *'GO!'*

■ **398** *'SLOWER.'*

Communication ■ 399

A long line is attached to a bottle
containing a message. The bottle is
thrown in the tug's wake where it will drift
back and alongside the boat being towed.

■ **399** *Communication under tow*

■ **400** *Towing under sail*

Towing under sail ■ 400

Prepare the towline and carry one end forward on the windward side.

Approach the boat to be towed on her leeward side.

Pass over the towline as you cross her bow.

Fall off quickly, as the tension on the line will tend to bring you up into the wind.

NOTE:

Towing under sail can be surprisingly effective. Even larger craft can be towed in this fashion, especially on a reach, broad reach, and downwind.

Towing a school of dinghies ■ 401

Stream a heavy warp with a float at the end.

The dinghies are attached with a slipped stopper knot (rolling hitch).

■ **401** *Towing a school of dinghies*

Towing a grounded or stranded craft

If a towline cannot be heaved or taken over by a dinghy then from upwind or upcurrent, a bight can be floated over attached to a lifejacket, jerry can, fender or mooring buoy.

A long scope should be used.

To prevent falling off beam-on to the stranded boat, a bow anchor can be set. Winching in the anchor cable, together with the force of the engine and sails, will yield maximum pulling power.

For the boat being towed

The towline

This should be made fast to:

The strongest point on the foredeck. On Samson posts and bollards, attach the warp with a tugboat hitch ■ **402.**

The mast at deck level, if it is stepped on the keel.

A bight around the coach roof and/or the cockpit winches ■ **403.**

A lashing joining the mast and both sets of shrouds.

■ **402** *A tugboat hitch*

■ **403** *Attaching the towline*

A set of oars or spars blocking the forward hatch ■ **404.**

Steer in the wake of the tug

■ **404** *Attaching the towline*

To prevent salvage claims

See: Salvage

Agree to a towing fee in advance.

Do not show any emergency or distress flags or signals.

Make the minimum use of warps or aid from the other boat. Merely the acceptance of a towline from another boat does *not* automatically entitle that boat to a salvage claim.

Make a detailed entry in the logbook and have the crew sign it.

In harbors and narrow waters

Towing alongside ■ **405, 406**

Both boats should be adequately protected by fenders. **See: Fenders**

The towboat should approach on the lee side of the boat being towed.

■ **405** *Towing alongside*

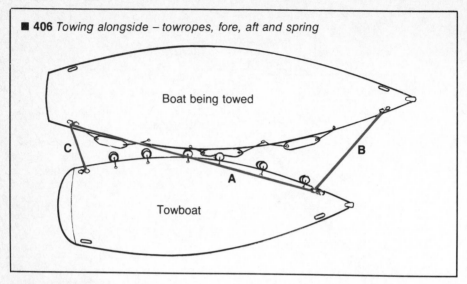

■ 406 *Towing alongside – towropes, fore, aft and spring*

Boat being towed

C

B

A

Towboat

Attach lines **■ 406:**

A strong warp from the towboat's bow – as a spring – to the stern of the boat being towed **■ 406A.**

From the bow of the towboat to the bow of the boat being towed **■ 406B.**

From the stern of the towboat to the stern of the boat being towed **■ 406C.**

All lines should be tied as tightly as possible to bind both boats into a single unit.

NOTE:

For maximum steering the rudders of both boats should be used.

WARNING:

Because of the great increase in mass the backing and stopping power of the towboat's engine will be greatly reduced.

Towing from a dinghy ■ 407

The warp should be of some floating rope material.

Length: long enough so that it just rises out of the water with each pull from the dinghy.

If too long, force will be lost in friction.

If too short, the rope will jerk with each pull.

■ 407 *Towing from a dinghy*

■ **408** *Towing with an outboard*

Towing with an outboard ■ 408

The dinghy must be attached to the quarter of the boat being towed.

Attach lines:

From the bow of the dinghy to the stern of the boat being towed.

From the stern of the dinghy to the stern of the boat being towed.

From the bow of the dinghy to the forward quarter of the boat being towed.

The dinghy will only provide thrust. The boat must be steered.

Towing from shore ■ 409

The towrope should *not* be fastened to the stem, even if someone is at the helm. The boat will still have a strong tendency to sheer shorewards.

Instead, the towrope should be fastened somewhere near the mast, a chain plate, for example, which is usually just forward of the center of pivot.

If there are obstacles between the path and the boat, the towrope should be looped around the mast, then hoisted to the hounds to clear the obstacle.

■ **409 Towing from shore**

Tranquilizers

See also: Pain killers

Tranquilizers can separate the perception of pain from the reaction to pain. By calming the sensation of pain, the reaction becomes less severe.

Valium (available in England, France, Germany and the U.S.), is usually effective in a dosage of 5–10mg. every 6 hours.

NOTE:

When taking tranquilizers, do *not* drink alcohol.

	Dosage
England	
Piriton	4mg. 3–4 times/ day
France	
Polaramine	2mg. 3–4 times/ day
Germany	
Tavegil	1mg. 3–4 times/ day
U.S.	
Benadryl	50mg. 3–4 times/ day

Tropical jellyfish stings

Treatment

Using gloves or rags for protection, remove any tentacles at once.

Treat for shock if necessary. **See: Shock**

Wash the area with fresh water and well-diluted ammonia.

Coat the area with a bicarbonate of soda paste.

Administer an antihistamine.

Turnbuckles

See: Rigging failure

Typhoons

See: Law of storms

U

Urine

In survival conditions

Urine should *not* be drunk. It will not replace lost body fluids.

More than likely, urine will become concentrated, turn dark and be painful to pass. However, this is not harmful.

In emergencies urine can be used as an antiseptic.

V

Vitamins

The four major vitamins

1 – Vitamin A

A deficiency results in

Night blindness.

Dry, flaky skin.

Brittle, falling hair.

A susceptibility to infectious diseases.

Common sources of vitamin A are

Green vegetables (particularly watercress and parsley), carrots and apricots.

Cod liver oil.

Whole milk.

2 – B complex

A deficiency results in

Nervousness.

Fatigue.

Headaches.

Insomnia.

Gas and constipation.

Common sources of B complex vitamins are

Whole grain foods.

Milk and yogurt.

Liver.

Leafy green vegetables.

Brewer's yeast.

3 – Vitamin C

A deficiency results in

General fatigue.

Mild depression.

Headaches and aching limbs.

Eventually scurvy. **See: Scurvy**

Common sources of vitamin C are

Nearly every fresh vegetable and fruit, especially citrus fruits.

4 – Vitamin D

A deficiency results in

Poor absorption of calcium and phosphorus, which are essential for strong bones and teeth.

Common sources of vitamin D are

Milk and butter.

Eggs.

Fish oils.

Fresh green vegetables.

W

Water

At sea, fresh water can be obtained from

Rainwater collection. **See: Rainwater**

A solar still. **See: Solar still**

Distillation. **See: Distillation**

Taking on water

Use your own hose, if possible.

NOTE:

To prevent the growth of bacteria, after each use the hose should be drained, dried and plugged.

If using someone else's hose, flush it out for at least a full minute.

Purification

Foul water in tanks is sometimes made palatable by addition of $1/4$ to $1/2$ box of baking soda through a filter pipe.

Household bleach

For clear water, two drops per quart or liter.

For cloudy water, four drops per quart or liter.

2% tincture of iodine

For clear water, five drops per quart or liter.

For cloudy water, 10 drops per quart or liter.

Let the water stand for at least a half hour before using.

Pouring the water back and forth between containers will aerate and remove much of the chlorine smell.

Weather forecast

Barometer

Stable: stable weather.

Rising slowly: good weather ahead.

Falling slowly: wind, and a further, faster fall.

Falling quickly: (more than one millibar per hour) stormy weather.

Chapman's rules

A few general rules are often helpful. First, *foul* weather is usually forecast by a *falling* barometer with winds from the *east* quadrants; *clearing* and *fair* weather usually forecast by winds shifting to *west* quadrants with a *rising* barometer. Second, there are the rules formerly printed on every U.S. National Weather Service daily surface weather map:

'When the wind sets in from points between south and southeast and the barometer falls steadily, a storm is approaching from the west or northwest, and its center will pass near or north of the observer within 12 to 24 hours, with the wind shifting to northwest by way of south and southwest.

'When the wind sets in from points between east and northeast and the barometer falls steadily, a storm is approaching from the south or southwest, and its center will pass near or to the south of the observer within 12 to 24 hours, with the wind shifting to northwest by way of north.

'The rapidity of the storm's approach and its intensity will be indicated by the rate and amount of fall in the barometer.'

'Long foretold, long last;
Short warning, soon past.'

Temperature

A normal curve

Rising in the morning, then falling again after noon: good weather.

In summer

Quickly rising temperature: good weather.
Quickly falling temperature: bad weather.

In winter

Quickly rising temperature: bad weather.
Quickly falling temperature: good weather.

Wind

A sudden change in direction after several days of constant wind means bad weather.

An increasing wind in the morning, and a decreasing wind in the afternoon means good weather.

An increasing wind in the afternoon or evening means storm and rain.

The wind following the sun, that is, from the east in the morning and from the west in the evening means good weather.

The wind 'backing' against the sun, until it is east in the evening means bad weather.

Clouds

Clouds in layers and at different levels means changeable weather.

Cumulus in the morning and less in the afternoon and evening means bad weather.

Gathering altostratus clouds means an approaching warm front with rain.

Spotted altocumulus means continued good weather.

'Mares' tails' with little motion means gales from the direction they radiate from.

Sunrise

Red: bad weather.

Clear, but with a reddish touch: bad weather.

Sunset

Red: good weather.

Clear behind cumulus clouds: good weather.

Bright yellow: wind.

Pale yellow or green: rain.

Moon

Silver and light: good weather.

A ring or halo: wind and rain.

Sea life

Sea birds far out to sea: good weather.

Sea birds flying inland: bad weather.

Vast quantities of jelly fish: good weather.

Porpoises in shallow water: bad weather.

Phosphorescent sea: good weather.

See: Law of storms

Wind

See: Law of storms, weather forecast

Wood repair

For cracks or holes in

plywood hulls ■ 410, 411

Cut the damaged area into a square hole.

Cut a marine plywood plug – preferably the same thickness as the hull – to fit the hole exactly.

Cut a backing plate at least 2in. (5cm.) larger than the hole on all sides.

Glue (epoxy) and screw/nail the backing plate to the inside of the hull. For larger holes battens should be used instead of a backing plate.

Glue and screw/nail the plug into place.

For additional strength a layer of fiberglass can be molded over the backing plate. **See: Fiberglass repair**

NOTE:

Since the two outside layers of marine plywood are the hardest (those with the dark grain), they should not be sanded too much.

■ 412

■ 413

■ 410 *Repairing a plywood hull*

■ 411 *Repairing a plywood hull*

For cracks or holes in planked hulls

Patches ■ 412

Cut a wooden patch which will overlap the damaged area by at least 4in. (10cm.)

Cover the inside of the patch with mastic, bedding compound, or sealer. If none is available, a rag, towel, or sailcloth well greased or soaked in paint, primer or asphalt will serve as well.

Screw or nail the patch in place, carefully sealing the leading edges.

NOTE:

For irregular surfaces, such as those found on a clinker hull, a tingle may have to be used. This can be cut from sheet lead or copper and easily beaten into shape. The tingle is screwed or nailed in place in the same manner as a patch ■ 413.

For cracks, weak, damaged or leaky areas

Fiberglass

Materials

See: Fiberglass repair

Procedure

NOTE:

Fiberglass will form a secure bond with wood, but only if the wooden surface is carefully prepared.

Remove any old paint or varnish. Paint remover or sanding is the best method. Burning off old paint is likely to drive oils into the wood which may prevent a strong bond. The final surface should be smooth, but not overly so. All sharp edges should be rounded in order to prevent air bubbles from forming under the mat.

Paint the bare wood with enough coats of activated resin to fill in the grain. Let the area dry, then sand it lightly.

Cut the cloth or mat to fit the area. Several layers will be necessary, and their weave patterns should be criss-crossed.

Wet the first layer thoroughly with resin. Before it begins to cure, add the next layer. Use a roller or bottle to squeeze out any air bubbles which would become weak points.

Add one or two additional coats of resin to fill in the pores of the last layer and provide a smooth finish.

Wire rope clips

See: Bulldog clamps

Wounds

Three immediate dangers

Bleeding. **See: Hemorrhages**

Shock. **See: Shock**

Infection which could lead to blood poisoning.

Treatment

Stop the bleeding by applying a sterile dressing. This should not be too tight. If firm at first to stop the bleeding, it should be loosened later.

If possible, elevate the injured part.

Do not

Touch it.

Leave it exposed to the air.

Remove any glass or metal fragments unless they are superficial and can be easily lifted out.

If the wound is large and open

Hold it closed with a plaster or pack it with sterile gauze. After the bleeding has stopped, with clean hands, sew it closed with a sterilized sail needle (the smallest one available). **See: Sterilization**

If the wound is deep and gaping, stitch the flesh together with catgut, then close the skin with silk. Holding the needle with forceps or pliers, make one stitch at a time, tying off each one with a granny knot. Clip off the ends.

NOTE:

Sewing a wound closed is usually not unbearably painful. It is normal that quite a bit of blood will flow while the sewing is taking place.

If the wound is closed, such as a bruise

Salt-water compresses will have a soothing effect and reduce swelling. But they should *not* be used for open wounds.

The Medicine Chest

Whatever it's called—the ship's medicine chest, the surgeon's chest, the small bottom drawer in the galley with necessary first-aid items, even the first-aid mini-kit in the hiker's backpack—the collection of supplies you may someday need to ease pain, get a crew member back into working shape, or even save a life is important. A boat, no matter what size, should always be equipped with a clearly marked first-aid kit.

The medicine chest or first-aid kit should be in a secure place on the boat, where it is accessible and yet where rainwater will not damage it or the contents. All persons aboard should know its location. In many cases duplicates of certain elements, such as aspirin or Band-aids, should be kept in another part of the boat, because of their common use for minor ailments. Make sure that the main contents of the first-aid kit are not depleted just before a more important need arises.

Medicines grow stale. Scissors and other instruments rust. These items should be inspected several times a season, and certainly before the start of any long voyage.

Obviously, the size of the boat, the duration and conditions of the voyage, the skill and knowledge of the skipper or crew, all have a bearing on the contents of the medicine chest.

At the end of this chapter is a list of first-aid supplies. Final selection depends on the type of voyage.

Voyages to faraway ports call for extra information beyond the condensed information in this book. If you can't take a doctor as a crew member, here is a list of useful medicine-chest books:

Advanced First Aid Afloat, by Peter F. Eastman, M.D., published by Cornell Maritime Press.

Medical Emergencies at Sea, by William Kessler, M.D., published by Hearst Marine Books.

Standard First Aid and *Advanced First Aid,* published by the American Red Cross.

The Cruising Sailor's Medical Guide, by Nicholas C. Leone, M.D., and Elisabeth C. Phillips, R.N., published by David C. McKay Company.

The Ship's Medicine Chest and Medical Aid at Sea, published by the U.S. Department of Health and Welfare.

Handbook of the Hospital Corps (NAVMED-P-5004), published by the U.S. Government Printing Office.

There is also a service that provides emergency medical information on the radiotelephone, through an 800 number (hotline). "Medical advice can be as close as your marine radio," according to the Boat Owners Association of the United States. This service has been available to U.S. merchant seamen since 1981 from MAS, Inc. (Medical Advisory Systems). Now it is available for pleasure boats. BOAT/US members are enrolled in a subgroup called MMAS for a nominal annual charge (about $6). Using the VHF or SSB marine radio, a boat owner can call the hotline of MMAS, and talk directly to a licensed physician (available on a 24-hour basis). The doctor will answer questions, make recommendations, and can give emergency step-by-step instructions. In addition, for a onetime extra charge (about $17) your medical history can be kept on file to help the doctors develop a working diagnosis and to alert them to any problems in your medical background that could affect their emergency treatment plan. For information on BOAT/US membership and the MMAS service, write Boat Owners Association of the U.S. at 880 South Pickett Street, Alexandria, VA 22304.

Various specific medical emergencies are listed in the main text of this book. Following are some general principles, adapted from the U.S. Coast Guard folder "First Aid for the Boatman."

The four things to think of first, after someone is injured, are:

1 – Check and clear the airway, so the patient can breathe freely.
2 – Stop the bleeding.
3 – Protect the wound.
4 – Treat for shock.

Long before any illness or accident involves first aid or medical treatment, there are some specific guidelines to keep in mind:

Have everything you may need readily available.

Keep calm. Don't act excited; don't let events confuse you.

Act quickly, with efficiency and confidence, making decisions on priorities as soon as possible.

Mistakes to avoid:

In applying a pressure point or tourniquet, use only enough pressure to stop the bleeding.

On burns, do not break blisters, remove shreds of tissue, or apply additional home medications. Do not remove charred clothing that sticks to a severe burn. Do not apply ice water.

Do not try to give fluids to an unconscious person.

If in doubt about a fracture, treat the injury as though it is a fracture. Splint the injured limb at once, not after moving the victim.

If in doubt about shock, remember that there are a variety of signs, and they may not all appear in every casualty. Some of the symptoms:

1 – The eyes may be glassy or lackluster; and pupils are dilated or suggest fear and apprehension.

2 – Breathing may be normal, rapid, or labored.

3 – The lips may be pale or cyanotic (bluish gray).

4 – The skin may be very pale or a peculiar ashen gray (if dark complected).

5 – The skin temperature may be lowered and the body covered with a clammy sweat.

6 – The pulse may be nearly normal or it may be rapid, weak, thready, and of poor volume.

7 – There may be retching (trying to vomit), nausea, vomiting, hiccups, and dryness of the mouth, lips, and tongue.

8 – Restlessness and apprehension are common signs.

9 – Veins in the skin are collapsed. Veins normally visible at the front of the elbow or forearm, and the backs of the hands, may become invisible.

10 – Complaints of thirst are common. Shock victims may complain of thirst rather than pain even when severely wounded.

Keep the victim lying down and maintain normal body temperature. If there is a delay in obtaining medical care, giving the victim water, preferably with ½ level teaspoonful each of salt and baking soda, is recommended. An adult should be given 4 ounces every 15 minutes, a child approximately 2 ounces and an infant about 1 ounce.

Choking on food is an accident that can happen aboard a boat. The victim will be unable to breathe or even groan. He may give the choking sign: clutching the throat, or pointing to it.

If the victim is coughing or otherwise trying to expel the foreign matter, initially it is best not to interfere with these efforts. Don't strike him on the back. Don't question him needlessly. Be calm and encourage him to cough. If the victim's own expulsion efforts are not successful he may become semiconscious or unconscious from lack of oxygen. Roll him on his side and deliver a firm blow with the heel of your hand over the victim's spine and between his shoulder blades.

The Heimlich maneuver (or technique) is a method of treating choking victims. The rescuer stands behind the victim, puts both arms around him just above the beltline, and allows the victim's head, arms, and upper torso to hang forward. Then the rescuer grasps his own wrist and quickly thrusts into the victim's abdomen—a strong, rapid hug—so that the diaphragm is forced up. This compresses the lungs and expels residual air in them. The foreign object will often pop out of the victim's windpipe like a cork from a wine bottle. If the victim is lying down, sit astride the victim's lower torso or buttocks and perform the hug in the same way as for the standing victim. If the victim is lying on his back, sit astride the pelvis, place one hand over the other, and forcefully thrust into the upper abdominal region. If a second person is available, he should be ready to remove the foreign matter from the victim's mouth. If the victim vomits, his mouth should be immediately cleaned out by turning his head to one side and cleaning the mouth with your fingers or a cloth.

Prevention: Knowing what kinds of accidents and injuries happen aboard boats is useful in setting up a "risk management" control system.

The medical and safety director of the Offshore Racing Commission, Dr. Matt Houghton, advocates obstruction-free cockpits, with protruding switches replaced by rocker devices and energy-absorbing padding in appropriate places. He has found that hand bruises, back compression, rib and lung contusions, cardiac contusions, burns, kidney contusions, twisted knees, and lower lips lacerated by teeth are common injuries.

The dangers of hypothermia and the techniques of cold water survival also come under the risk management category.

A person falling into the water gasps (but can rarely shout), breathes rapidly, and has less ability than usual to hold his breath. So keeping the head out of the water is a must—one more reason for wearing a proper Personal Flotation Device. In addition, the PFD, like clothing, helps prevent the loss of body heat.

Hypothermia, the lowering of the body temperature, occurs 20 to 30 times faster in water than in air, says Richard Hiscock in his *Safety Notes for Fishermen*. Keeping the head out of the water helps minimize the danger of rapid reduction of body temperature. Avoiding movement, including swimming, also helps prevent additional heat loss.

HELP is the acronym for the Heat-Escape-Lessening Posture. Hold your upper arms against your sides with the wrists placed over the chest. Your legs should be drawn up as close as possible to the chest, with ankles crossed. If you are wearing a PFD this posture prevents high heat loss of the head, neck, sides, and groin.

If there are other persons in the water, assume the Huddle Position. All survivors face inward, with the sides and chests close together and arms around each other. Either the HELP or the Huddle Position will increase survival time by as much as 50%.

When water temperatures are below 60° F., float coats or anti-exposure coveralls are recommended. Many lives have been saved by the one-piece dry exposure (survival) suit. Certain exposure suits, approved by the U.S. Coast Guard, qualify as PFDs. They provide insulation as well as flotation.

Medicine chest supplies (not including prescriptions):

Absorbent cotton	Antihistamine tablets
Ace elastic bandage	Anti-itch ointment
Adhesive tape	Aspirin (or pain-killing equivalent)
Alcohol (rubbing)	Bacitracin ointment

Bandages, in 1in., 2in., and 3in. sizes
Bicarbonate of soda
Butterfly closures
Catheter
Dental kit
Enema bag or Fleet enema
Epsom salts (magnesium sulfate)
Forceps or tweezers
Gauze, sterile, in 4in. by 4in. squares
Hot-water bottle
Hypodermic syringes
Kaopectate or Pepto-Bismol
Laxative
Milk of Magnesia
Peroxide

Resusitube (plastic airway for mouth-to-mouth resuscitation)
Safety pins
Scissors
Seasickness medicine (Marezine, Dramamine, etc.)
Sling
Snakebite kit
Splints
Sutures or Steri-Strips
Thermometer
Tincture of green soap
Tongue depressors
Tourniquet
Vaseline

Prescription medicines can be a special problem. Doctors who are themselves experienced in boating realize that antibiotics, ready for an illness that may never happen, pain-killers on hand for an accidental injury that may never occur, and extra supplies of a crew member's special medication are all customary and necessary on a cruising boat that may be days or weeks from standard medical assistance.

So, for all except the smallest boat, in order to have proper supplies aboard for cruising it may well be necessary to talk with a knowledgeable doctor. He can write a prescription or under some circumstances provide you with special supplies. It may be suggested that dangerous drugs be kept under lock and key. The idea may come up of having a couple of prescriptions written in advance—if someone aboard expects to be in a port with a pharmacy.

As medical knowledge changes, the names of favored drugs also change. Instead of trying to specify the brand name of a pain-killer, ask your doctor which type of analgesic he suggests. Depending on the circumstances, he may prescribe antibiotics or other special emergency drugs. He may suggest one of the azosulfas for urinary tract infections and a tetracycline because of the broad-spectrum usefulness. In the main body of the text of this book, under "antibiotics" and under "antiseptics," you will find the English, French, and German names and related details such as dosages for certain drugs, but this information is presented as an extra; your own physician's instructions are the most important. There are specialized antibiotics for skin infections and eye infections and various medicines for other specialized problems, like intestinal flu, dysentery, or "Montezuma's revenge." A doctor who has some boating and travel experience is the best kind to know.

Index

Wind/Barometer Table

Weather tendencies are best observed over an extended period – indeed, a single observation of local conditions rarely gives much useful information for the future. One of the best ways to follow weather patterns is by correlating your barometer's readings (adjusted to sea level) with the local wind. Barometric readings should be taken every hour on a regular basis to determine the tendency up or down, discounting minor fluctuations that represent regular daily change in pressure: In most parts of the country, a barometer will read at its highest about 1000 and 2200 each day, at its lowest about 0400 and 1600. Variation from minimum to maximum is normal if it is within .05 inch in each 6-hour cycle.

Wind Direction Quadrant	Barometric Reading	Tendency	Coming Weather Pattern
SW to NW	30.10–30.20	Steady	Fair, slight temperature changes for next day or two
SW to NW	30.10–30.20	Rising fast	Fair, rain following within two days
SW to NW	30.20 and higher	Steady	Continued fair, no sizable temperature change
SW to NW	30.20 and higher	Falling slowly	Fair for next two days; slowly rising temperature
S to SE	30.20–30.10	Falling slowly	Rain inside 24 hours
S to SE	30.20–30.10	Falling fast	Rain 12 to 24 hours ahead; wind increasing
SE to NE	30.20–30.10	Falling slowly	Rain in 12–18 hours
SE to NE	30.20–30.10	Falling fast	Rain within 12 hours; increasing wind
E to NE	30.10 and higher	Falling slowly	Summer: Possibly no rain for a few days Winter: Rain within 24 hours
E to NE	30.10 and higher	Falling fast	Summer: Rain within 12 hours Winter: Probably rain or snow and increasing winds
SE to NE	30.00 or lower	Falling slowly	Rain continuing a day or two
SE to NE	30.00 or lower	Falling fast	Rain and high winds, clearing and cooler within 36 hours
S to SW	30.00 or lower	Rising slowly	Clearing; Fair for several days
S to E	29.80 or lower	Falling fast	Storm; Clearing and colder in 24 hours
E to N	29.80 or lower	Falling fast	Severe storm from NE
Turning W	29.80 or lower	Rising fast	Clearing and colder